# *The Four Middos*

◆ ◆ ◆

Reflections of *Mussar* according to the teachings of our Sages *z'l*

◆ ◆ ◆

Reviewed and translated by
Divine mercy granted to
Nissim Elharrar

◆ ◆ ◆

In Jerusalem holy city, to be rebuilt nowadays, *Amen!*
*Kislev 5781*

Editing and translation:

Elharrar Maxime
P.O.B. 16124
9116101 Jerusalem
Israel

Phone number: + 972.545.238.233

Notes and corrections are
welcome by email:

peleyoets@gmail.com

ISBN 978-2-9557018-6-7

First edition in English translated from French

Printed by Amazon

In order to help spread this book, you may offer
it on the occasion of a *simha* or in memory of
a loved one and obtain it via:

www.peleyoets.com

© 2021 – All rights reserved to the translator and his
descendants by any type of process or support

מכון וישיבה ע"ש הגאון
החיד"א זצ"ל
ע.ר. 580068369

Hanida Institute for Research of the Talmud
H'IDA
& Seminary for Rabbis and Rabbinical Judges

גאון עוזנו הרב
חיים יוסף דוד
אזולאי זיע"א

כולל אברכים
כולל בעלי בתים
כולל ערב
עזרה לנזקקים
שיעורי תורה לציבור

הכתובת:
רח' בית וגן 44
ת"ד 16096
ירושלים 91160
טלפקס 02-6414415
נייד 052-3801304

Address:
44 Bayit Vagan st.
P.O.B. 16096
Jerusalem 91160
Call. 972-523801304
Tel. & Fax:
972-2-6414415

בס"ד ל' סיון תשע"ח

# הסכמה

בא לפני האברך החשוב הרב נסים מקסים אלחרר שליט"א עם גליונות מספרו החדש "ארבע מידות" המבוסס על פרק מתוך ספר "שערי קדושה" למרן ר' חיים ויטאל זיע"א.

עברתי בין ביתריו וראיתי מלאכת איש סופר מהיר שכתב פרקי הגות ומחשבה המדריך לעבודת ה', וכל מטרתו לזכות את הרבים בעבודת ה' יתברך.

הספר נכתב בלשון צרפתית כדי שירוץ הקורא בו למען דעת ה' ולעובדו בלבב שלם.

והנני מברכו שחפץ ה' בידו יצלח ויתברך בכל הברכות כולם וזכות הרב זיע"א תגן בעדו ובעד בני ביתו אמן.

בברכת התורה,
הדורש שלומכם וטובתכם
הרב ניסים הררי שליט"א

מכון וישיבה
ע"ש הגאון חיד"א זצ"ל
ע"ר 580068369

## Letter of approval
## from Rabbi Yosef Mizrachi shlita

Dear Rabbi Nissim Elharrar,

I want to compliment you on your book "The Four Middos". You did an outstanding job, I bless you that it will be published to as many people as possible.

And may you continue with your *Avodat ha Kodesh* and publish many more important books as well.

With appreciation,

Rabbi Yosef Mizrachi
Monsey NY

## Table of Contents

## *Introduction*

Blessed be *Hashem* who has granted us the privilege of sharing time with those who live in the *Bais Hamidrash* and to thus have the merit of being surrounded by Torah scholars, from whom we draw so much vitality and *chizuk.*

During the course of our study of tractate *Taanis* with our *Rav shlita,* many of the *aggados* therein have awakened in us inspirations that we humbly wish to share with you.

The present world in which we live, is immersed in a sea of self-centeredness and materialism that has resulted in our forgetting the essential foundations of the Torah, and has impeded our having an unlimited *emunah* in *Hakodosh Boruch Hu.* This has led us to falsely believe that modernism and science with all their "novelties and discoveries" contain the keys to happiness, and thus may be the best way to live.

The Torah, however is eternal, always relevant and never outdated. This knowledge has led to the tremendous rise of the study of Torah, not only here in *Eretz Yisroel,* but throughout the world! Many "highly educated" people have put everything aside to return to their "true heritage" by linking to our *Source of Life.* King Solomon, in his great wisdom, taught us about the Torah in *Mishlei* (ch3. 17-18): *Her ways are ways of pleasantness, and all her paths are peace. She is a tree of life to those who grasp her, and her supporters are praiseworthy.*

The Torah way of life, *Torat Chaim,* is the best way for people to develop and flourish. The Torah is not, as some ignorant people would like to claim, a long list of forbidding prohibitions. Did not King David already say (Tehillim 34-9): *Taste and see that the Lord is good.*

Why would the Creator, create rules contrary to our nature? After all, He created our nature! Embedding ourselves in the ways of Torah is really the only way to ensure our happiness. We humbly express the wish that the ideas that we discuss in this collection of thoughts will bring us a little closer to *Hakodosh Boruch Hu,* remove us from the vanities of this world and increase *Shalom* (peace) and *Ahavah* (love) amongst us, *Amen!*

We wish to warmly thank Dr. Yaakov Sharbit *shlita,* for the French version, and Rav Moshe Chaliwa *shlita,* for the English version, for agreeing to review this work, *Leshem Shamaim.* May *Hashem* fill them in this world with all the *Berachos* of the Torah, with the *Keren Kayemet (principal) L'olam Habah! Amen!*

With all of the blessings of the Torah.

## *Description*

The "Rokeach" teaches us that an "Or Haganuz[1]" illuminated the world for 36 hours from the birth of *Adam Harishon* until he left *Gan Eden.* This corresponds to the total of 36 lights of *Chanukah* (without the *shamash),* reminding us that we must have a proper vision of the world around us, according to our holy Torah.

In his book "Shaare Kedusha", Rabbi Chaim Vital *z'l* tells us in the name of Ari *z'l,* the four principal *Middos Tovos* (good character traits) and the four principal *Middos*

1 ***Or Haganuz:*** *And God said: "Let there be light." And there was light. And God saw the light, that it was good;* (Bereshis 1-3 and 4). Rashi explains that *Hakodosh Boruch Hu* saw that the villains of the flood generation would take advantage of "the light", so he set it aside for use by the *Tzadikim* for the time to come (Chagigah 12a), as the *Possuk* tells us (Job 38-15): *But from the wicked their light is withheld.* The Talmud explains in the name of Rabbi Elazar (Chagigah 12a), that this light allows man to see everything, to observe everything from one end of the world to the other, without limit, even through the walls. What allows us to see? It is the light. It allows our eyes to perceive the world around us. However, this vision is limited. What we see is limited to the maximum capability of what our eyes can observe. For example, when looking at the sea, infinity is the maximum point on the horizon that we can see. However, thanks to *Or Haganuz,* we could see endlessly, without a material barrier, from one end of the world to the other. This means that we see through the light that illuminates us, and not through our eyes, which are actually just light sensors. Kabbalah teaches us that every object around us is composed of soul and matter. If this object were without soul, but only composed of matter, we could not see it, it would be invisible, because it would be lifeless. Indeed, this soul is static, without vitality, but present and essential to the reality of things.

*Raos* (bad traits) that are related to the four letters of the divine Name, *Yod Kei Vav Kei.*

We will begin by noting the four *Middos Raos* that outrage the divine Name:

1. *Yod: gaavah,* pride
2. *Kei: diburim betelim,* useless words
3. *Vav: taavos,* the desire for physical pleasures
4. *Kei: atsvus,* sadness

In contrast, the four *Middos Tovos* that glorify the divine Name:

1. *Yod: anovoh,* humility
2. *Kei: shtikah,* silence
3. *Vav: mius betaanuguei haguf,* the revulsion of physical pleasures (when it is not being used for a *mitzvah)*
4. *Kei: simcha tmidis bechelko,* to be constantly happy with his portion

Those who are in possession of the four good *Middos* become a *Merkava Leshem Havaya* (a residence for divine Providence). Such a person has perfectly fulfilled his *Tikun* (the repair of his being in this world), because he is the proper receptacle for receiving Torah, he is in sync with the four letters of the Tetragrammaton. *Hashem* is looking for this kind of person in this world to reside there, as the *Possuk* tells us (Shemos 25-8): *And let them make Me a sanctuary, that I may dwell among them.* It is in the heart of the person that the *Shechinah* dwells in, as the *Possuk* tells us (Devarim 23-15): *For Hashem your God walks in the midst of your camp.* The Zohar explains that the heart (center of your being) is the place of residence of divine Providence, for those who are fitting to receive it, in accordance with the rest of the verse: *so your camp shall be holy,* devoid of bad thoughts. When man behaves in accordance with the Torah, he becomes fit to become a receptacle of *Kedusha* (holiness).

We will now, with the help of *Hashem,* attempt to deal with each *Middah.*

## *Yod: gaavah, pride*

Rabbi Moshe Cordovero in his book "Tomer Dvora" teaches us that *anovoh,* humility, is the best character trait. Its opposite, *gaavah,* pride, is consequently the worst character trait.

King Jeroboam (Kings 1), caused all the people of Israel to sin. Nevertheless, *Hakodosh Boruch Hu* gave him a last chance. (Kings 1 13-33): *After this incident Jeroboam returned not from his evil way.* The Talmud (Sanhedrin 102a) reports that *Hashem* pulled Jeroboam by his coat and said to him: "Give up your misbehavior, and I and you and Ben Ishay will walk together in Gan Eden". Jeroboam asked *Hashem:* "Who will lead?" *Hashem* replied: "Ben Ishay will lead". "If that's so, I do not want to". His pride made him lose his future world.

A derivative of pride is jealousy. Cain was jealous of his brother Hevel when Hevel's offering was accepted by *Hashem* and not his, as the *Possuk* tells us (*Bereshis* 4-5): *but to Cain and to his offering He did not turn; this angered Cain exceedingly.* The aftermath was tragic (verse 8): ...*Cain rose up against Hevel his brother, and slew him.* Rashi explains: "He started by looking for a quarrel, in order to find an excuse to kill him". He was also jealous of the fact that twin sisters (who were to become his wives) were born with Hevel, while Cain was born with only one sister.

Korach was also jealous of Moshe and Aaron (Bamidbar 16). His jealousy led him to the point of enlisting 250 great personalities of the People of Israel against our master Moshe (verse 3): *It is too much for you, seeing all the congregation are holy, every one of them, and the Lord is among them; why do you exalt yourselves over the assembly of the Lord?* Their end was tragic (verse 32): *And the earth opened her mouth and swallowed them up, and their households, and all the men who were with Korach, and all their goods.*

Rabbi Eliezer Papo, in his book "Pele Yoetz", reports on the subject of pride:

The great evil of arrogance is explicit in the words of our Sages in the Talmud, Midrashim, and in all of the holy books. Is it insignificant that which is written (Mishlei 16-5): *All arrogance of the heart is an abomination unto Hashem.* Our Sages said (Sotah 5a): "Anyone who displays arrogance will be excommunicated". He is considered as one who worshiped idolatry, had multiple illicit relationships, his dust will not be resurrected, and many other such dreadful things. Everyone knows the great evil of haughtiness, but the problem is that people think the essence of haughtiness is a person who walks completely upright and moves his arms here and there. No one really knows what arrogance is! However, there is a sign – from the "son" one can recognize the "father". Being overly demanding, angry, etc. are the "children" of arrogance. If there are no "fathers", from where do the "progeny" come? In fact the evil inclination has become so strong that he shows a person that being overly demanding, complaining and angry are the perfection of character. So much so, that people say that someone who does not react in such a manner is not a man!

The hair of a man who is God fearing and pure-hearted will stand on end from seeing the severity and enormous evil of haughtiness, and his heart will be elated when he sees the tremendous praise of humility. A man must strive with all of his power and pure thoughts to recognize his own minimal value, be lowly in his own eyes, and that he should be of those who are insulted by all men, even the members of his own family, and does not strike back, get angry, or complain at all. He should only be very, very humble and submissive! Continuous reading of the works of moral perfection and fulfillment of the verse (Tehillim 51-5): *and my sin is in front of me at all times, are* critical. Even a person who has achieved great wisdom and knowledge must recognize that intellectual achievement is secondary, everything is judged according to the majority of one's actions. A man is evaluated for what he is – the scale of justice is in the hands of *Hashem*. A person must realize that despite his position, knowledge, intellect, capabilities, and the kindnesses that his Creator has bestowed upon him, he has not discharged even one part in a thousand of his obligation, as *Koheles* teaches us (1-18): *For with much wisdom comes much grief.* One must increase his understanding and distress as he recognizes that he has not done what he should have, and he has not endeavored to achieve that which he could have. Ultimate justice is *Hashem's!* (Man will be judged in the future world on the use made of the capabilities which *Hashem* put in him, and on the tasks which he could have carried out relative to his potential.)

A man should judge every person favorably. Even if he sees with his own eyes and his heart clearly discerns that his friend, wife, or even his student or employee has sinned against him and acted inappropriately, it is fitting that he should not get angry, pained, or upset at all. For what should a living man complain? Each man for his sins! Behold, *Hashem* told him to curse! A person must think what difference does it make if someone honors or dishonors him? Everything is vanity and futile pursuit!

In truth, relative to the great reward reserved for those who are insulted, his "friend" has bestowed upon him a great kindness, and it is fitting for a person to rejoice over those who insulted him even more than those who honored him. His only regret should be that his friend has committed a sin and caused grief and imperfection in Heaven. Therefore, a person should take measures to prevent his friend from sinning against him and encroaching upon him. If they have wronged him, he should attempt to admonish them, when he knows his words might be accepted. He should pursue venues which will encourage them to apologize, to correct their wrongful ways, and that they should sin no more. Everything must be done in a proper manner, so that there will not be even the slightest allegation of wrongdoing or desecration of *Hashem's* name, Heaven forbid. Every astute individual will act with wisdom and balance his words with justice according to the nature of the person, the place, and the need of the hour. If the situation requires fear, let him demonstrate anger and disapproval. However, his heart should be dispassionate within him, and all of his actions should be for the sake of Heaven. *Hashem* will not withhold good from those who walk with integrity. Our Sages recommended as a protective device to avoid arrogance, he should flee from honor, and, all the more so, should not seek fame...

During a *drasha* on "the ego" in the summer of 5774 in *Har Shmuel,* we learned from Rabbi Binyamin Sharabi *shlita* the following notions:

The secret of the relationship with your colleague is in the understanding that he is not perfect and that we do not have to expect him to be perfect in his behavior, because everyone has come into this world to perfect oneself in divine service, to improve and correct one's character traits. If we blame him without taking great precautions, the result will be a face-to-face confrontation. People of our generation are not ready to hear and accept reproaches directly. We must use an educational method adapted to the style of our time. The best way to have good relationships with your wife, children, family, friends and everyone, is to highlight the moral and spiritual qualities of the person, to compliment them on their good character traits, in aspiration of boosting their ego.

Everyone has a well-developed, sometimes oversized ego. Direct confrontation will not yield any positive results.

With ones spouse, it will result in arguments, useless words that we will regret, often and surely "lashon hara"; with children, unnecessary insolent reactions; with family, a certain distancing will occur; with friends, until the relationship breaks down. In conclusion, even if we are entirely right, let us be the wise man and not the one who is right. Therefore, when we have a message to pass, we will begin by praising our colleague and in the middle or at the end of our compliments, we will add a hint of what the person should correct in his personality or behavior.

Our master *Moshe Rabbeinu, olov ha Sholom,* in the *Parasha of Devarim,* out of respect for the *Bnei Yisroel,* only reproached them with allusion. Rashi (verse 1) explains that the Torah listed all the places where they irritated *Hakodosh Boruch Hu,* thus reminding them of their misdeeds by simple allusion, in order to lead them to question themselves and to do *teshuvah.*

Our holy Torah uses only gentle ways. Similarly, we have a duty to resemble it in our behavior towards others. Patience is the best advise in this kind of situation. Always keep in mind that *Hashem* can wait seventy years for a person to correct himself. What right do we have in this case to be impatient and demand from the other an immediate reaction to our remarks? Rabbi Akiva, when he was still only the shepherd Akiva, saw that a drop of water had dented a rock, he understood that even he could start studying Torah at 40 years old and become Rabbi Akiva, teacher of 24,000 students!

On the borderline of pride, we have the gate of anger, may *Hashem* preserve us from it. The "Pele Yoetz" advises the angry, in order to begin to get rid of this bad trait, to engage in a war against it. He recommends using the following tricks on him: study and put in writing daily the teachings of our Sages (Talmud, Midrashim, Zohar, Ari *z'l)* on this subject and repeat them to reinforce the good inclination over the bad. If this is not enough, force yourself to pay a fine (which may be donated, for example, to *tzedakah)* on each fit of anger, force yourself to a day of fasting. If he still can't control his anger, make up your mind to shut up anyway, like a deaf-mute. And if he speaks, it should be in a low voice and in a conciliatory-manner, even if his heart is in turmoil, his anger will be abated. It is well known that the bad trait of anger leads to many others, such as the fire of discord and curses, etc., may *Hashem* preserve us. Silence in the face of anger is like water that extinguishes fire...

### *A continuous presence of the Torah before the eyes*

Rabbi Oshaya (Taanis 7a) asks why is the Torah compared to water, wine and milk? He answers according to the verse (Isaiah 55-1) : *Ho, everyone who is thirsty go to the water, even one with no money, go, buy and eat; go and buy wine and milk without money and without price.*

The Talmud teaches us that just like these three drinks can only be stored in the most ordinary utensil (clay), so only the humble one will remember the Torah he learned. The Talmud (Taanis 7b) continues that just like water, wine and milk can deteriorate in an instant if we do not pay enough attention to it (Rashi explains because of their liquid consistency, anything that is mixed in them makes them immediately unfit for consumption, unlike oil and honey which are thick, we can remove anything that falls in them without throwing everything away), in the same way Torah which was acquired by study can be forgotten in the blink of an eye. Rashi explains that we forget it if we don't revise it constantly.

The verse says (Mishlei 23-5) : *Will you cast your eyes upon it and it is gone...* Rashi explains (Megillah 18b and Berachos 5a): "If you stop your eyes from being fixed on the Torah, it will be erased from your memory in a blink of an eye". The "Pele Yoetz" keeps repeating that our whole purpose on earth is to provide satisfaction to *Hakodosh Boruch Hu* by studying Torah and practicing *mitzvos.* Having occupations that have no use for our daily life or our income, like reading magazines or surfing the internet, in short, wasting such precious time that will never come back, is causing us considerable and priceless losses. Our favorite occupation should rather be the accumulation of knowledge in Torah and the application of its *mitzvos;* as opposed to the constant search for vain pleasures in this world, which will never satisfy us and which have no purpose. Can we acquire time in order to recover the time that was lost in vain? Each moment of our life takes on a whole new dimension.

The *Chazon Ish,* in his book "Emunah and Bitochon", reports that our nature is infected by that of the *Serpent,* due to the misdeed between him and Chava (Eve). If we don't try to correct ourselves daily, we'll have all the *bad Middos* (character traits). A Jew who stagnates is a Jew who recedes; we must constantly aspire to evolve upwards.

On this subject, the *Kli Yakar* wonders about the repetition of language of the verse (Bereshis 25-19): *And these are the generations of Isaac, Abraham's son: Abraham begot Isaac.*

If Isaac is the son of Abraham, it is clear that Isaac was begotten by Abraham?!

In verse 12, the Torah states: *Now these are the generations of Ishmael, Abraham's son, whom Hagar the Egyptian, Sarah's handmaid, bore unto Abraham.* In this verse, Ishmael's parentage is specified by the father and mother, while for Isaac, Abraham is the only one cited.

In Hebrew, there is a difference between the son *(Ben)* and the child *(Yeled)*. The son is one who has acquired good character traits through Torah learning and influence of his father or his master, such as mercy, good manners, etc. The child is the one who inherited them. Ishmael is the son of Abraham, as the pupils are the sons of the teacher, but he is also the child of the Egyptian Hagar, which means coming from the country where debauchery dominated, as the *Possuk* tells us (Bereshis 21-9): *And Sarah saw the son of Hagar the Egyptian, whom she had borne unto Abraham, mocking.* Rashi explains: "mocking *(metsachek):* this is adultery, as the *Possuk* tells us (Bereshis 39, 17): *And she spoke unto him according to these words, saying: "The Hebrew servant, whom you brought to us, came to me to mock me (letsachek)".* Hagar was on a very high spiritual level, but she was the daughter of Pharaoh, the king of Egypt. We deduce that Ishmael, through his mother, received by inheritance very bad character traits (according to Rashi of the same verse: idolatry, adultery and murder). In addition, Ishmael was not influenced by his father's good behavior nor did he follow his teachings, this on his own, since ultimately he decided to deviate from the right path. This is why the Torah relates him to his mother, Hagar the Egyptian.

Let's go back to Isaac: *Kli Yakar* tells us that he received the nature of Abraham and followed his teachings, which is why Abraham is cited both as his father and as the one who fathered him. On this subject, Isaac was modest to the point of having waited until forty years old to marry his *zivug* Rivkah, unlike his brother Ishmael, son of Hagar the Egyptian, infatuated with debauchery. Isaac did not want to marry a *Canaanite* woman, a people from Cham (who mutilated his father Noah), from whom they inherited debauchery. An only son from such a family was not lacking marriage proposals, how could he have waited so long, if not for the reason previously mentioned.

*Kli Yakar* goes on to explain the reason why Isaac (who came from such a pure source) had a son like Essav (who raped married women, stole and killed). The Torah specifies that Rivkah was the daughter of Betuel, from Aram's territory, Lavan's sister. The boys generally resemble the mother's brothers, which is why one of his sons, Essav, received the nature of his uncle Lavan, the scammer. His grandfather Betuel, deflowered all the virgin women of his country before their marriage (*Yalkut Shimoni* 109, we learn this from his name: *betulim* in Hebrew means virginity). The people of Aram territory were also "gluttonous", as Abraham noted, he also prayed not to be part of such a country. We now understand the origin of Essav's tendencies, the disbeliever, rapist, thief, killer and glutton. We know that Essav studied Torah, but he did so out of greed for knowledge, and not to correct and dominate himself.

Torah is called *Torat tavlin* (Torah of spices). Its study (in our case the *Mussar)* allows us to forge a second personality, to perfect and correct our original nature, infected by many faults, instigated by our bad inclination *(Yetser Hara).* If we stagnate, we retreat, and our primary nature takes precedence over our second nature. We must therefore be constantly in a dynamic of improvement, leaving no respite to our original nature, suffocating it for good.

We can ask ourselves the question: "For what purpose did *Hakodosh Boruch Hu* create man like this?" The answer is: "In order to give him a higher wage and more reward". Man is forced to fight against himself all his life, constantly seeking to improve, in honor of *Hashem,* blessed be He, by studying the Torah and practicing *mitzvos,* thus perfecting his relationship between himself and *Hashem,* between himself and his neighbor. It would be cruel on the part of *Hashem* to leave us on earth if we were perfect. The goal of our coming into this world is mainly to repair our personality through the study of Torah, the correcting of our relationship with *Hashem* (through our divine service) and the propagation of good to correct the relationship with our neighbor, as the *Mishna* teaches us (Avos 1-2): "The world stands on three pillars: Torah, divine service and the spread of good".

### ***Kei: diburim betelim, useless words***

Speech is the distinctive attribute of the human species. This distinction places him at the top of *Hakodosh Boruch Hu's* creative work.

Speech is creative, *Hakodosh Boruch Hu* created the world with ten words (Bereshis 1). Rabbi Dovid Abudraham, who was the pupil of the *Tur,* son of the *Rosh,* reports in his book "Sefer Abudraham", the relationship between the ten utterances of the Creation and the addition of *Tehillim* in *Shabbos* morning prayer:

There is an allusion in these psalms to the ten utterances with which the world was created:

The verse (Tehillim 105-1): *O give thanks unto the Lord, call upon His name,* הוֹדוּ לַה' קִרְאוּ בִשְׁמוֹ, included the ten words of Creation.

The verse (Tehillim 19-2): *The heavens declare the glory of Hashem,* הַשָּׁמַיִם מְסַפְּרִים כְּבוֹד אֵל, comes to recall the first utterance which is (Bereshis 1-1): *In the beginning Hashem created the heaven and the earth,* בְּרֵאשִׁית בָּרָא אֱלֹהִים אֵת הַשָּׁמַיִם וְאֵת הָאָרֶץ.

The verse (Tehillim 33-1): *Rejoice in the Lord, O ye righteous, praise is fitting for the upright,* רַנְּנוּ צַדִּיקִים בַּה, comes to recall the second utterance which is (Bereshis 1-3): *Let there be light!* יְהִי אוֹר, which was created at the beginning for the *Tzadikim,* then put in reserve in their use for the times to come (see note 1, subject Description).

The verse (Tehillim 34-1): *A Psalm of David; when he changed his demeanour before Abimelech, who drove him away, and he departed,* לְדָוִד בְּשַׁנּוֹתוֹ אֶת טַעְמוֹ לִפְנֵי אֲבִימֶלֶךְ וַיְגָרְשֵׁהוּ וַיֵּלַךְ, comes to recall the third utterance (Bereshis 1-6): *Let there be a firmament,* יְהִי רָקִיעַ, during the separation between the waters below and the waters above as a result of them being expelled by *Hashem.*

The verse (Tehillim 90-1): *A Prayer of Moses,* תְּפִלָּה לְמֹשֶׁה, comes to recall the fourth utterance (Bereshis 1-9): *And Hashem said: "Let the waters under the heaven be gathered together unto one place, and let the dry land appear",* יִקָּווּ הַמַּיִם מִתַּחַת הַשָּׁמַיִם אֶל מָקוֹם אֶחָד וְתֵרָאֶה הַיַּבָּשָׁה, as well as (Tehillim 90-16): *May your works be visible to your servants,* יֵרָאֶה אֶל עֲבָדֶיךָ פָעֳלֶךָ, recalling the appearance of the soil.

The verse (Tehillim 91-1): *Who sits in the refuge of the most high, he shall dwell in the shadow of the Almighty,* יֹשֵׁב בְּסֵתֶר עֶלְיוֹן בְּצֵל שַׁדַּי יִתְלוֹנָן, comes to recall the fifth utterance (Bereshis 1-11): *And Hashem said: "Let the earth put forth grass",* תַּדְשֵׁא הָאָרֶץ דֶּשֶׁא, reminding us that He created plants to nourish us and shelter us under their shade.

The verses (Tehillim 135-1 and 2): *Halleluyah! Praise the name of the Lord; give praise, O you servants of the Lord, you that stand in the house of the Lord,* הַלְלוּיָהּ שֶׁעֹמְדִים בְּבֵית ה׳ בְּחַצְרוֹת בֵּית אֱלֹהֵינוּ, come to recall the sixth utterance (Bereshis 1-14): *Let there be lights in the firmament,* יְהִי מְאֹרֹת, coming to remember that He created them to serve Him in His courts. "Stand" in the sense of being available, as the *Possuk* tells us (Bereshis 18-8): *and he stood by them.*

The verse (Tehillim 98-1): *A Psalm. Sing the Lord a new song,* מִזְמוֹר שִׁירוּ לַה׳ שִׁיר חָדָשׁ, comes to recall the seventh utterance (Bereshis 1-20): *Let the waters swarm,* יִשְׁרְצוּ הַמַּיִם, as well as (Tehillim 98-7): *Let the sea roar, and the fullness thereof; the world, and they that dwell therein,* יִרְעַם הַיָּם וּמְלֹאוֹ, which corresponds to (continuation of verse 1): *for He has done marvelous things,* כִּי נִפְלָאוֹת עָשָׂה.

The verse (Tehillim 121-1): *A Song of Ascents. I will lift up my eyes unto the mountains,* שִׁיר לַמַּעֲלוֹת אֶשָּׂא עֵינַי אֶל-הֶהָרִים, comes to recall the eighth utterance (Bereshis 1-24): *Let the earth bring forth the living creature,* תּוֹצֵא הָאָרֶץ נֶפֶשׁ, as well as (Tehillim 121-3): *He will not allow your foot to falter,* אַל יִתֵּן לַמּוֹט רַגְלֶךָ, meaning: although man will eat herbs that will keep him alive, it is possible that his feet will falter without force to move, if he does not eat meat.

The verse (Tehillim 124-1): *A Song of Ascents; of David. If it had not been the Lord who was for us,* שִׁיר הַמַּעֲלוֹת לְדָוִד לוּלֵי ה׳ שֶׁהָיָה לָנוּ, comes to recall the ninth utterance

(Bereshis 1-26): *Let us make man,* נַעֲשֶׂה אָדָם, that corresponds to (Tehillim 124-2): *If it had not been the Lord who was for us,* לוּלֵי ה׳ שֶׁהָיָה לָנוּ, if He had not made us in His image, we would have been like animals.

The verse (Tehillim 136-1): *O give thanks unto the Lord, for He is good,* הוֹדוּ לַה׳ כִּי טוֹב, comes to recall the tenth utterance (Bereshis 1-28): *Be fruitful, and multiply,* פְּרוּ וּרְבוּ, so that the good men and the *Tzadikim* come into the world to pay homage to Him. The rest of the verse is (Tehillim 136-1): *His mercy endures for ever,* כִּי לְעוֹלָם חַסְדּוֹ, that corresponds to (Tehillim 89-3) : *For I have said: 'The world is built on kindness',* עוֹלָם חֶסֶד יִבָּנֶה, corresponding to: *Be fruitful, and multiply.*

The verse (Tehillim 92-1) : *A Psalm, a Song. For the Shabbos day,* מִזְמוֹר שִׁיר לְיוֹם הַשַּׁבָּת, comes to remember the seventh day, when *Hashem* rested there from all work.

Rabbi Yaakov Dwek in his book "Derech Emunah" reports on the subject of useless words (subject: Gossiping) the following things:

The author of the book "Chemdat Yamim" draws our attention to the behavior of these people who meet in public places, talk about the accomplishments of kings and the wars they wage, report that in such places were found princes, decree that this is good for the king of the south, that for the king of the north, announce as a certainty that evil will come from the north, affirm that if so and so had acted in such and such a way he would have won it over his rival... These people take pleasure in talking about everything, even if their words are the fruit of their imagination and are far from reality; such speeches are not only useless, but can be harmful in one way or another. These people, he notes, waste their time on trivialities; in their conversations, they learn to lie, to flatter, to mock and deceive.

When they have finished speaking about the princes of the different nations, they start to *rant about* the country, the food, the economy and the high cost of living, all things that they understand nothing about and that give them endless opportunities to speak badly and spark outrage.

After having discussed politics, the conversation continues by gliding imperceptibly towards backbiting. One tells the other how much, with all the respect he owes to such and such a person, he is surprised that he is able to afford so much luxury and that he deprives himself of nothing, as well as the quality of his servants which prove the point. The other, then may be tempted to reply: "What is it to you, if such and such a person lives; so it is, there are people who amass fortunes by dishonest means, without bothering, while you and I just earn enough to feed us". Critics don't stop there. One begins to say that such a person constantly creates trouble for him, takes nothing into consideration, he is "hard like cedar and inflexible like oak" and the other goes on to say that he has the same problems with this individual, but that he doesn't know if he should talk to him about it. He ends up admitting that he can no longer hold back, that he must express himself, even if it means slandering and thus committing an unforgivable fault. It is out of affection for him and because he wants to avoid disappointment that he will reveal to him what will have to remain a secret between them... After this preamble that we often hear, the tongue loosens and backbiting does not know limits. Given the gravity of the latter, it makes its author lose, in the blink of an eye, his share in the future world.

Under the subject "Unworthy words", Rabbi Yaakov Dwek writes:

*Kabbalists* teach that every man can speak a certain number of words during his lifetime and if he talks a lot, he risks shortening his life. Rabbi Chaim Vital, in his introduction to "Etz Chaim", writes that every word spoken is a part of the person that departs from him. This can be seen in some patients who enter a coma that makes them mute for days before they die, simply because they have run out of words. They compounded their case with futile words and words that they should never have said. It is in this sense that he explains the verse of Ecclesiastes: "Do not let your mouth fault against your flesh and do not say before the divine messenger that you are not like a divine messenger capable of serving *Hashem* permanently, that it was an error. Why should Hashem be angered by your speech and destroy the work of your hands." By such language, you would only irritate *Hashem* and cause Him to interfere with your activities. You do not make an effort for *Hashem* and you abandon the Torah, favoring the futile at the expense of the essential. Do you believe that *Hashem* bothered to create man only to eat, drink and walk? It wouldn't be very logical".

Rabbi Yaakov Dwek continues under the subject "Social Justice":

In *Mishna Avos,* Rabbi Yossi Ben Yochanan, who was from Jerusalem, tells us: "Let your house be wide open and the poor be the people of your house"; he means: certainly, your house must be open to all the needy who come to solicit you; however, you should know that you have a special duty to help those in your house, your family, who are in need.

Rabbi Yossi continues and asks us not to talk too much with "the woman"; he may mean that the husband should not tell his wife too much about how much he gives to his loved ones. Indeed, it often happens that women are mean and envious of their husbands' relatives. If, in addition, the husband tells his wife that he is helping them, the latter could come to prevent him from being generous towards them, claiming that they drink and eat inordinately like bears, waste their money, do not know how to manage their property and that giving them money would be futile, especially since they would have acquired it without effort... If a man follows such advice, he opens the doors of hell.

In addition, one who comes to the aid of others to have something to boast about, not only does he not receive a reward for his gesture, but in addition deserves punishment, because there is no fault more serious than bragging and pride and, if we are motivated in the way we react, we cause immense harm (end of quote).

In view of the teachings of our Sages, we should have our hair standing on its end, regarding speaking vain words, spoken especially during *Shabbos,* considered by the *Zohar* as a transgression of this holy day, entirely reserved for the delights of *Shabbos* and, mainly in Torah study. Whoever wants to devote himself to doing the will of *Hashem* will be helped from Heaven in order to speak only words necessary for his existence or that of those around him. He will prolong his life by speaking as many Torah words as possible, so that the promise of the verse can be fulfilled (Devarim 11-21) : *That your days may be multiplied, and the days of your children...*

### *Rainwater*

Rabbi Akiva, seeing the drops of water penetrating a rock, understood that the Torah would gradually penetrate his heart.

This is the best method for doing *teshuvah:* strengthening yourself in Torah study by learning something and repeating it until you absorb it, then move on to another subject. To remember your study, repeat it as much as possible. The Talmud teaches us that a hundred and one times is not like a hundred repetitions. Each revision brings its share of novelties. In addition, it facilitates understanding. The *Chida* teaches us that an angel helps us better understand what we repeat, depending on the intensity of our.

The Talmud (Taanis 6a) teaches us that the first rain comes to warn people to prepare for winter, such as repairing their roofs, bringing in dried fruits from the fields, etc. The Talmud continues, according to Rabbi Nehilay bar Idi in the name of Shmuel, that when the rain does not fall, *Bnei Yisroel* do *teshuvah,* fast and give *tzedakah* (according to Rashi). At the *Bais Hamidrash* of Rabbi Yishmael, we learn that the last rains come to boost the growth of the wheat, thus obtaining a good harvest. A lack of rain at this time ends in great losses. *Hakodosh Boruch Hu* therefore warns or cautions us through nature's behavior.

The Talmud continues by telling us that if it does not rain on three consecutive dates until the end of the month of *cheshvan,* which is the deadline for the start of the rains (although scholars in Torah have already fasted for this purpose), the Rabbinical Court decrees to the community three fasts from the second day of the month of *kislev.*

Water is essential for our life in this world. A lack of water is a dramatic factor in all areas. Nowadays, we are less afraid of droughts, because we rely on our own strength, such as seawater desalination plants or groundwater pumping, waiting for better days... Not such a long time ago, such means did not exist and the conclusion was unfortunately not to expect too much.

*Hashem* could grow nature without water, without rain. The fact that the rain does not come in its time indicates an obligation to question ourselves, to make a deep examination of conscience, to correct us, in order to return (to do *teshuvah)* towards *Hashem.* "Modern technology" with its weather flashes every hour on the radio, falsely make us believe that the seasons behave according to "natural" rules, discovered by "scientists", according to learned calculations, thus distancing us from our attachment to *Hashem* and to have our eyes constantly focused on Him. The Talmud comes to give us proof to the contrary, *Hakodosh Boruch Hu* uses nature to send us a message: if our behavior is not adequate to the rules of Torah, we must correct ourselves as soon as possible, the rain hasn't fallen yet!

The days of public fasting were divided into three periods (Taanis 12b). In the morning until noon, Rashi explains that the Community met and made a deep examination of conscience by asking everyone if there was no theft in their hands, because theft is one of the reasons causing the drought. If there was, the theft was returned and the injured parties were appeased. The afternoon was divided into two parts: during the first period we read the Torah (Shemos 32: *Moses implored... And the Lord repented of the evil which He said He would do unto His people)* also Prophets (Isaiah 55: *Seek the Lord while He may be found, call upon Him while He is near; Let the wicked forsake his way, and the man of iniquity his thoughts; and let him return unto the Lord, and He will have compassion upon him, and to our God, for He will abundantly pardon.)*, and during the second period, we poured out our hearts in prayer (Nehemiah 9: *...the children of Israel were assembled in fasting... they stood and confessed their sins, and the iniquities of their fathers... And they stood in their place, and read in the book of the Law of the Lord their God a quarter of the day; and another quarter they confessed, and prostrated themselves before the Lord their God)*.

The Talmud reports many other situations that cause drought. Taking this lesson forward, why does the increase in the number of patients in hospitals not awaken us all, let us examine our conscience? Instead of being proud of our state-of-the-art hospitals, we should be asking ourselves the real questions. The Talmud reports that if three people die in the same city, one after the other, the whole city must fast. We are far from this reality. *Hakodosh Boruch Hu* speaks to us through the events of our life, but unfortunately, the lack of knowledge in Torah and the abuse of secular knowledge have veiled our eyes with a barrier that prevents a look worthy of our holy Torah, to focus on statistics of health or life expectancy... Let's focus on the prayer of Channah (Samuel 1-2):*...neither is there any rock like our God.. Hashem brings death and gives life; He brings down to the grave, and brings up. The Lord makes poor, and makes rich; He humbles and He elevates.*

The Talmud gives us other signs of drought, as the *Possuk* tells us (Devarim 11-17): *and He shut up the heaven, so that there shall be no rain* – וְעָצַר – that the morning clouds are inconsistence, as the *Possuk* tells us (Hosea 6-4):*...your goodness is as a morning cloud... (The Prophet was expressing the fact of their empty acts of kindness.)* This verse makes us aware of how delicate *Hashem* is when He communicates with us. He treats our goodness as a *morning cloud,* without any consistency, like those clouds of which no rain comes to fertilize the earth.

Rav Yehuda (Taanis 6b) teaches us that rain is the "husband" of the earth, as the *Possuk* tells us (Isaiah 55-10): *For as the rain comes down and the snow from heaven, and will not return there, rather it waters the earth and causes it to produce and sprout, and give seed to the sower and bread to the eater;*

The *Gaon of Vilna* in the name of our Sages *z'l* reports that the rain has a special blessing to fertilize the earth, as the *Possuk* tells us (Bereshis 1-7): *the waters which were above,* to produce a better crop, without toxins, with better taste. We have proof of this from the milk given by cows grazing in the mountains at the beginning of spring, by the quality and taste of their milk, unique at that time.

Rav Yehuda says (Taanis 7a) that a rainy day is as great as the day of the Torah gift at Mount Sinai. The Maharsha writes that the Torah is good for the soul as water is good for the body. Each one gives vitality to what corresponds to it. Rain is formed from the waters below (tachtonim) with the waters above (elyonim) from the sky (Bereshis 1-7), meaning that the rain is the product of the link (kesher) between the two different waters of the sky. Just as when *Hakodosh Boruch Hu* came down to earth on the day of the Torah gift, a link (kesher) was formed between the world above (elyonim) and the world below (tachtonim). It's a day to feel closer to *Hashem,* blessed be He.

## *Vav: taavos, the greed of physical pleasures*

*Hakodosh Boruch Hu* created man with five senses: vision, smell, taste, hearing and touch.

The body is the means for man to serve his Creator, that is why He trained him with all the functions necessary for this duty. However, man can be mistaken in using this wonderful body. The sage will take advantage of this world in order to sanctify matter, for the glory of *Hashem.* The fool is in the constant search for the vain pleasures of this world. He imagines a life of pleasure in all areas is the purpose of its existence.

The "Sefer Chareidim" details positive *mitzvos* that we can apply with our senses:

With vision, we can apply the *mitzvah* to look at the *Tsitsis,* as the *Possuk* tells us (Bamidbar 15-39): *that ye may look upon it, and remember all the commandments of Hashem.* The vision drives the memory and concretizes the realization of the *mitzvos.*

The Talmud (Gittin 60b) reports the *mitzvah* of *Shemos* 34-27: *Write these words for yourself,* that it is not allowed to say them by heart, but to study them (the written Torah) from the book. For example, reading the *korbanos* (sacrifices) is considered to be the fulfillment of their offering[1].

1 On this subject, the Talmud (Megillah 31b) reports the *Midrash* that relates to us the conversation between *Hakodosh Boruch Hu* and

Another method of using our eyes for *Hashem's* service, is by crying after the departure of a *kosher* man (upright), as the *Possuk* tells us (Vayikra 10-6): *but let your brethren, the whole house of Israel, bewail the burning that Hashem has kindled;* also (Bereshis 23-2): *Abraham came to mourn for Sarah, and to weep for her.* Our Sages *z'l* said (Shabbos 105b) that one who does not shed tears on a *kosher* person will be punished by shedding it over his children, may *Hashem* preserve us from it. They also say that *Hakodosh Boruch Hu* counts and keeps in his Treasury every tear that has been shed, as the *Possuk* tells us (Tehillim 56-9): *You have counted my wanderings; place my tears in your bottle; are they not in your book?*

Many *mitzvos* are also linked to vision such as: getting up at the sight of a Sage, checking the food for any presence of worms or insects, the blessing on the moon, the sun, the rainbow, etc.

Regarding negative *mitzvos,* the "Sefer Chareidim" reports:

---

*Avraham Avinu.* Our patriarch asks *Hashem* (Bereshis 15-8): *Hashem-Elokim,* how will I know that I am in possession of it? Rashi explains that Avraham wanted to know how the people of Israel should be forgiven for their faults in order to inherit the land of Israel. *Hashem* replied that they must offer sacrifices in order to obtain their forgiveness. Avraham asked, "I understand when the *Bais Hamikdosh* is present, but in its absence, what will it be?" "Hashem replies: "I prescribed them a *korbanos* (sacrifice) *seder* (order), each time they read it, I consider it as if they were offering Me a sacrifice and forgive them all their faults". **Reading this Midrash, we understand the need to start the *Shachrit* (morning) prayer from the beginning and not from "Hodu". Fifteen minutes that make all the difference...**

Regarding vision, it is written (Bamidbar 15-39): *and you shall not explore after your heart and after your eyes, after which you stray.* We have been warned here not to look at a married woman or one of the other prohibitions linked to debauchery, at the risk of succumbing to it. A woman must also protect her eyes from all shameless, forbidden looks.

Pride can also depend on the eyes, as the *Possuk* tells us (Tehillim 101-5): *who so is haughty of eye and proud of heart, him I cannot bear.*

The Torah forbade us to contemplate the worship of idols, as the *Possuk* tells us (Vayikra 19-4): *Turn not to the idols...*

*Then you shall guard against anything evil...* (Devarim 23-10): this verse comes to warn us not to look at nudity, even without intention of seduction (taking advantage only of its beauty). In the verse: *and that you shall not explore after your own heart and your own eyes,* we are forbidden to look in a direction of debauchery.

On the subject of smell, the ban on smelling a woman's perfume is part of *Even Haezer's* rules to "get away from debauchery" (21). A married or even single woman should not wear perfume when she is away from home or among an assembly where there are men. She must keep this attribute in order to find favor only with her husband. *Pele Yoetz* teaches us that smell allows us the opportunity to pronounce many blessings on scents. If it comes from a tree, "Boireh atsei bessomim" (who creates aromatic shrubs). If it is a product of the earth and its root is renewed from year to year, "Boireh isbei bessomim" (who creates aromatic herbs). If it doesn't come from the tree or the earth, "Boireh minei bessomim" (who creates all kinds of aromatics).

The tongue is the organ of taste and is found in the mouth, the opening through which so many things enter and leave. On the subject "Eating and drinking", *Pele Yoetz* reports:

There are three categories when eating and drinking: *mitzvah,* permitted, and prohibited. A person has the ability to create all of his meals into a meal of a *mitzvah,* if he meets all of these conditions that are said in truth by the Sages, from whose mouth we live. First, one needs to intend through his eating that he be healthy and strong for the sake of the service of *Hashem,* may His Name be blessed, and be like "The person who is good to his soul, is a man of kindness (Mishlei 11-17)". This means that he must refine and bring to light all of the sparks of holiness that are attached to everything that he eats. He also needs to pray for his sustenance before eating. It is an immense obligation, as it is explained in the Zohar...

Behold, the person who delves into the holy book "Reishit Chochma", will see with his own eyes that the intentions associated with eating are identical in their importance as offering sacrifices (note: which were offered at the Temple to forgive our faults in order to satisfy Hashem). Fortunate is one born of a woman who achieves the building of the upper realms by his eating, on condition that he directs his heart to Heaven, and performs these things according to custom, law, and with purity of hands...

Likewise, a person needs to be careful to eat for the satisfaction of his soul, and should not gorge himself so that his stomach is bulging from excessive eating. In such a case, his satiation is tantamount to wickedness. Whoever "crawls" upon his belly, i.e. eats voraciously, builds a habitation for the evil inclination. The *Mekubalim* (mystics) wrote that whatever one enjoys of this physical world that is more than necessary for the satisfaction of his essential needs, adds strength to the "side" of evil and encourages his evil inclination to overpower him. Surely, a person who indulges in excessive meals and social parties gives great power to the "side" of evil. Just as a *mitzvah* which is done by many people together elevates and increases the might of the Heavenly host, so too transgressions done by the many together is horrific and increases the influence of the "side" of evil. The Sages of moral excellence already wrote that one who eats for more than his basic needs commits several wrongdoings: 1) He violates the prohibition of wanton destruction of his food. 2) He wastes time in eating and relieving. 3) If his stomach is upset and he requires frequent visits, he has again squandered time. 4) If he becomes sick and dies, he is culpable for his death.

Therefore, a man who cares for his life will distance himself from excessive eating and drinking. He will not eat unless he is hungry, and will not continue eating until completely satiated – just a little less. The *Raavad* wrote that one who withdraws his hand from food which he loves for the sake of the atonement of his wrongdoings is considered as if he fasted and is likened unto an altar of atonement. Behold, such is the astute individual who eats to satiate his soul and is considered like one who fasted. One who eats for the sake of Heaven should not pursue that which is pleasant to the palate but injurious to the body. Rather, he must prefer that which is beneficial to the body, even though it may not be so tasty to the palate. A person must be especially cautious in regards to excessive drinking of intoxicating beverages. It is a fire that consumes until it destroys – so many are its victims. Many people drank, "ravage" they drank, ravage and ruin visited their borders. It was bad for them, and bad for the world. Our Sages already strongly criticized them; especially in the case of a Torah sage, the pain will be much greater if he drinks too much and acts inappropriately among the masses. The Name of Heaven is desecrated by him. Fortunate is the intelligent man who acts judiciously in this regard... (End of quote.)

Making *Shabbos* a delight, by eating good meals with delicious dishes, is a *mitzvah* that reinforces good practice. This is the same for *Yom Tov* holidays and all meals taken on the occasion of a *seudas mitzvah* (like after a *Bris Mila* or a meal honoring the end of the study of a Talmud treaty, etc.).

The ear is the organ of hearing. Just as we have to be extremely vigilant with what we put in our mouth, so we have to be so with what we hear and listen to. These range from forbidden lyrics to forbidden songs.

Chofetz Chaim dealt extensively with the plague of backbiting, denunciation and slander. Only a daily study of the laws of *Shmirat Halashon* (literally guarding one's tongue) can protect us from these great sins and try to extricate them from our habits. **This is an absolute necessity for everyone, without any exceptions and without time limit.**

In the subject "Mourning", *Pele Yoetz* writes:

From this perspective one can hear how bad and awful are the actions of some men and women who gather together for a social party on *Motzaei Shabbos* or other nights, especially during the long winter nights. They engage in merriment of vanity, eating and drinking, playing music, and singing love ballads and Gentile songs. Woe unto them and woe upon them. Without a doubt their merriment will be transformed into grief – either in this world or the next, unless they repent. Because, besides the several prohibitions they violate, such as sitting with scoffers and improper speech in love songs, our Sages said (Sotah 48a), **"The ear that hears [inappropriate] songs will be uprooted"**. Thus, they are like a foolish son who angers his father and embitters his mother (Mishlei 17-25). The Holy One Blessed Be He says, "Woe! Cruel children! A voice is heard in *Ramah,* a wailing of bitter tears, Rachel is crying for her children. She is like a virgin wearing sackcloth. *Hashem* will roar from His high place, and from the seat of His holiness will raise His voice. He will surely roar over His abode, angels of peace will cry bitterly, all the host of heaven, the righteous, the pious, and the *Mashiach* cry and lament. All of this is for the Temple that was destroyed because of our sins. How can we at the very same time sit, sing, rejoice, and revel in a social party? This is nothing but an expression of apathy and blindness. Whenever a G-d fearing and kindhearted person hears such things, he will decide not to attend any such social gatherings or meals again and will not rejoice except in the joy of a *mitzvah* – the people of Israel will rejoice in its Maker. (End of quote.)

The psalm says (Tehillim 96): *O sing to the Lord a new song; sing to the Lord, all the earth. Sing to the Lord, bless be His name; proclaim His salvation from day to day. Declare His glory among the nations, His marvelous works among all the peoples. For great is the Lord, and highly to be praised...* We have a *mitzvah* of praising *Hashem* with the voice He has given us, singing pleasant songs in His honor, especially at the table on *Shabbos* and on *Yom Tov* holidays.

The body is a receptacle to be used to contain words of Torah in order to apply them. If we introduce things that are incompatible with the sanctity of the Torah, it leaves us at the speed of a blink of an eye. It's like a glass full of oil that is flushed out by the water you pour in. The story of Rabbi Yehoshua (Avot 2-8) is a case in point. The

*Mishna* says: “Rabbi Yehoshua, praiseworthy is she who gave birth to him!” Rabbi Ovadia mi Bartenura explains that during his mother’s pregnancy, she went from one *Bais Hamidrash* to another in her city asking the Elders to pray that her unborn child become a scholar in Torah. At birth, she left her baby’s cradle all day at the *Bais Hamidrash* so that he could only hear words of Torah. She thus caused her son to become one of the great Sages of the Torah, to the point that the *Mishna* praised the one who gave birth to him, so much he possessed good character traits.

If today so many children of good families leave the straight path of the Torah, it is often because of movies seen or music listened to which are incompatible with the sanctity of our precepts of life. One cannot claim a life of Torah, by behaving daily against its rules. Error is not permitted, because the consequences are immediate. The Jewish people are not like other peoples, they differ by its holiness and its modesty, as the *Possuk* tells us (Shemos 19-6): *and you shall be unto Me a kingdom of priests, and a holy nation...* Rashi explains: “Priests refers to princes, as in (Shmuel 11:8-18): *And David’s sons were priests (Kohanim)”.*

Each worthy Jew must stay away from the internet, television and especially smartphones. The internet is the biggest source of debauchery in the world today. All the knowledge that comes out of it, is in fact only a hook to attract and trap the visitor, sooner or later. Spending time chasing the news or the economy takes us away from having a busy mind in the Torah, which is our real purpose in this world. The Rabbinical Courts fill up divorce files, originating from an extra-marital meeting, following a visit on Facebook. The eyes see, the heart desires and the brain orders the body to act, may *Hashem* preserve us from it.

The skin is the organ of touch. It covers the whole body. It contains cells that allow us to perceive what we are touching. The Torah asks us to preserve our skin, as the *Possuk* tells us (Vayikra 19-28): *You shall not make any cuttings in your flesh for the dead, nor imprint any marks upon you: I am the Lord.*

The *shochet* (ritual slaughterer), before taking action, must, most importantly, check his knife, for fear of making the slaughtered animal unfit for consumption. This is done by passing the blade over one of the nails of his hand to assess its quality (or for some, on their tongue).

Caresses on the face are a wonderful way to express affection to children. The feeling of being loved builds them and gives them strength for life.

In the subject "Youth", Pele Yoetz writes:

And I comment on the words of our Masters *z'l* (Shabbos 152) on the verse (Koheles 11): *because adolescence and youth are futile,* by the things a man does during his youth, they darken his face during his old age. Rashi explains that it is about excessive intimate relationships.

But it also emerges from their words that if you are not careful enough to act properly when you are young, you will have to darken your face during old age to repair what has been altered. (End of quote.)

Our Sages have taught us to suppress our little organ, because the more you are satiated, it becomes the more demanding. The abuse of intimate relationships leads to premature aging of man, because the seed comes from the brain. The *Zohar* advises us to do the *mitzvah* of conjugal duty on Friday evening and on *Yom Tov* holiday evenings, before and after a trip, and of course on the evening of *tevila.* These are the best times to conceive holy *neshomos* (souls).

## *The key to happiness*

The Talmud (Taanis 5a) relates a series of questions that Rav Nachman poses to Rav Yitschak, regarding difficulties how to understand different verses of our holy Torah. Among these questions, there is one about the verse in Jeremiah (10-8) that raises deep reflection.

Rav Nachman does not understand the meaning of the verse:

**וּבְאַחַת, יִבְעֲרוּ** וְיִכְסָלוּ; מוּסַר הֲבָלִים, עֵץ הוּא.

(The rabbis translated: *They are altogether stupid and foolish: the vain (idols) for which they are punished, it is but wood.)*

The Talmud goes on to give a different explanation of the simple meaning *(Pshat)* of the verse:

Rav Yitschak reports what Rabbi Yochanan said about this verse: "It is a (interpretation of the word **וּבְאַחַת**) a sin which results in disbelievers **burning** (interpretation of the word **יִבְעֲרוּ**) in Hell. And what sin is it? *Avoda Zara* (serving idols, in its simple sense, in a deeper sense to perform acts which are foreign *(Zar)* to the divine Service)..." Rashi explains due to the sins they perform, the fools, who are disbelievers, will burn in Hell.

The following difficulties emerge from our study: is it only the transgression of *Avoda Zara's* that a person is condemned to Hell? Are there any prohibitions in the Torah whose transgression does not lead to Hell? What does the Talmud want us to understand?

The root of all sins, which man deliberately performs, is a kind of *Avoda Zara.* What kind of *Avoda Zara* is this? It is to draw vitality from a foreign thing *(Zar)* instead of drawing vitality *(Chayut)* by serving *Hakodosh Boruch Hu* by studying Torah and practicing *Mitzvos.* It is giving spiritual strength to a thing or deed that is not related to *Hashem.* We will try to give examples in the fields of prohibited acts and the (unrestrained) pursuit of pleasure *(Taavos),* in order to better understand.

When a person imagines that using deception (scams) or deceptive words in his business, earn him money, he gives vitality *(Chayut)* to the way he acts. He thinks that through this behavior, he is a successful trader in his business. He has, so to speak, taken the Master of the world out of the landscape, when we know very well that all our income comes from Him. To give *Chayut* to his deception is proof of his *Avoda Zara.* He thinks he is not provided for by *Hashem* (who has fixed our income since *Rosh Hashanah* for the whole year), but by imagining that it is his dishonesty. Unfortunately, its end has already been described by the prophet Jeremiah (17-11): *As the partridge that summons over young which she has not brought forth, so is he that amasses riches, unjustly; in the midst of his days it shall leave him, and at his end he shall be a fool.* Rav Yoram Abergel *zt'l* from Netivot taught us in a course on the sin of theft that the majority of the tests that man has to undergo in this world is his relationship with **money.** If we are convinced that everything that has to come to us, *Hakodosh Boruch Hu* will send it to us, how is it possible to act dishonestly? To ignore the fact that *Hashem* sees all our actions, hears all our words, knows all our thoughts, to do otherwise is to commit a sin. It is no coincidence that the prophet Chabakkuk said (2-4): וְצַדִּיק בֶּאֱמוּנָתוֹ יִחְיֶה – *but the righteous shall live by his faith.*

The Torah, its practice and its respect, is only a matter of *Emunah* (belief). If we are convinced that everything comes from *Hashem,* we will apply His Torah in its entirety, without transgressing anything. On the other hand, if we think that *Hakodosh Boruch Hu* only directs part of the things, or that we use our free will to act voluntarily, the door to sins is wide open.

In the search for pleasures *(Taavos),* we will begin by evoking that of impure thoughts (unlike a forbidden act that one is ashamed to do). When a man begins to think of foreign things *(zarim),* does he really imagine that the Master of the worlds does not know what he is thinking of at that time? *Hashem* examines the heart and probes the kidneys in order to know if we are serving Him with all our heart, with all our strength and with all our means (whether material or spiritual). Aside from the sin of deriving pleasure by having shameless thoughts, man derives vitality from it *(Chayut),* it is again a kind of *Avoda Zara.*

When a woman goes "shopping" every "Monday and Thursday", or when a person is constantly looking to taste new flavors, it is also a kind of *Avoda Zara,* instead they should draw vitality by serving *Hashem* in joy. Otherwise, they no longer have a taste for anything because they get their *Chayut* from their *Taavos. Boruch Hashem,* there is no shortage of *Mitzvos,* we are spoilt for choice!

*Hashem* is the Source of life *(Mekor haChaim),* in which case we should fill ourselves with vitality by serving Him in all our ways and activities, rather than abandoning Him to serve foreign gods, according to the verses (Jeremiah 2-11/13): *Has a nation ever exchanged its gods, though they are not gods? Yet My people has exchanged its glory for something of no avail... They have forsaken Me, the source of living waters, to dig for themselves cisterns, broken cisterns, that can hold no water.*

It is like the story of a man who had a stable and a well-paid job with a wealthy landlord with excellent social conditions. On a whim, he decides one day to resign from this job to go to work for a crook known to all, with very vague conditions!

The Talmud (Taanis 5b) teaches that the *Kuti* people served fire and the *Kedar* people water, although each of them knew that water extinguishes fire. Despite everything, they didn't trade their gods, *but My people has exchanged its glory for something of no avail...*

To live as a slave and dependent on your *Taavos* is to live under the roof of lies, of the virtual. It looks like a fool who bows down before the sun, believing that it will be of use to him. He depends on his *Avoda Zara* instead of depending on *Hashem.* The "Maharsha" teaches us that there are two errors with *Avoda Zara:* the first he abandons the Master of the world, the second, he serves something that will be of no use to him.

We can work, eat, dress, get married, have children, do sports, with the intention of serving *Hashem,* thus giving Him satisfaction. Sanctifying the material is to use our income (acquired honestly) to house us, eat *kosher,* send our children to true religious institutions, raise them in the path of the Torah, make *Shabbos* a delight, dress according to the rules of the *Tsnius,* buy books of Torah, give the *Maasser* (tithing to Torah scholars to strengthen the world of Torah), etc.

### *Kei : atsvus, sadness*

A famous parable says: "There was an unstable bridge in a city and many people fell into the river and drowned as they crossed over this bridge. The townspeople gathered and discussed what to do. They decided to raise funds to build a hospital next to the bridge!" The bridge represents Torah. We must strengthen ourselves in Torah study, have a solid foundation, so as not to fall. This world resembles a flooding river which sweeps away everything in its path. The bridge allows us to cross it safely. Not going in the ways of the Torah is an open door to falling in the river, may *Hashem* preserve us from it.

The evil inclination constantly pushes the man to fault. When he manages to knock him down, it doesn't stop there. He then trains him to despair, making him believe that he is worthless because of his bad deeds. He seeks to make him abandon the practice of Torah and *Mitzvos:* "What good is it, I am worth nothing!" One of the weapons of the evil inclination is causing man to forget. Man should never forget that *Hakodosh Boruch Hu* is waiting for everyone's repentance *(Teshuvah),* according to the verses (Ezekiel 18-31/32): *Cast away from you all your transgressions, which you have transgressed; and make yourselves a new heart and a new spirit; why should you die, O house of Israel? For I do not desire the death of him that dies, says the Lord God; turn yourselves back ( וְהָשִׁיבוּ), and live.*

Sadness leads man to despair, it is the open door to mental and physical illnesses, may *Hashem* protect us from it! If a person loses money, he is sad. The root of sadness is the lack of confidence in *Hashem (Emunah).* It is *Hashem* that limits us, there is no reason to be sad, He does it for our good. The following *Midrash,* reported by Rav Nissim Gaon from Kairuan, in his book "Sefer Maasiyos", illustrates this perfectly:

Rabbi Yehoshua ben Levy discovered during a study of the Torah something surprising and out of the ordinary to the point that the secrets of truth and righteousness were revealed to him. His difficulties in understanding had been resolved, having fasted for many days and praying to his Creator, blessed be He, that He would reveal the prophet Eliyahu to him.

*Eliyahu Hanavi* revealed himself to him and said: "What do you wish me to accomplish?" Rabbi Yehoshua replied, "I wish to accompany you and contemplate your actions in the world, this will be useful to me, so I can learn from you great wisdom." Eliyahu replied, "You will not be able to bear all that you will see from my actions and that will force you to ask the reasons for my actions." Rabbi Yehoshua replied, "Master, I will not ask, I will not annoy you with questions. My wish is to see how you act and proceed, no more." Eliyahu reaches an agreement with Rabbi Yehoshua: if he questions him in any way about his actions, he will no longer be able to accompany him. They started traveling together and arrived at the house of a destitute man who lacked everything. He only owned one cow which was his only source of income. This man and his wife were seated at the entrance of their house. They saw them arrive and walked towards them, greeted them and received them with much hospitality in the best part of their house. After rejoicing together, they shared their modest meal, drank, and spent the night in their house. The next morning, when they left, Eliyahu began to pray about their cow; she immediately fell dead. They started walking together, Rabbi Yehoshua was dismayed at what he had seen. He said to himself, "This is the reward for this pauper who received us so well, killing his only cow?" He asked Eliyahu: "Master, why did you kill the cow of this man who honored us so much?" Eliyahu replied: "Remember our agreement: do not question and only look. If you wish to separate from my company, I will tell you my reasons." Rabbi Yehoshua fell silent.

They traveled all day and arrived in the evening at the home of a wealthy man who did not pay attention to them. They stayed in his house without eating or drinking. This wealthy man had a collapsed wall in his house that needed to be rebuilt. The next morning, Eliyahu began to pray and built (miraculously) the wall. They resumed their journey together, Rabbi Yehoshua was again dismayed by Eliyahu's actions, but refrained from questioning him.

They traveled all day and arrived in the evening in a large synagogue, whose benches were made of gold and silver. Each member of the community sat very comfortably, according to their rank. One of them said, "Who will feed these needy people tonight?" Another replied, "Bread, water and salt will be more than enough here." They spent the night there, without being honored at all. The next morning, when they left, Eliyahu wished them that *Hashem* would make them all become leaders. They continued on their way all day, while Rabbi Yehoshua went from confusion to confusion, remaining silent.

At sunset, they arrived in another city. The locals came to meet them with great kindness, joy and courtesy. They rejoiced together and they were housed in their most beautiful home. They drank, ate, and spent the night very comfortably. In the morning, Eliyahu prayed and wished that *Hashem* appoints only one leader among them.

Hearing this, Rabbi Yehoshua could no longer hold back: "Now reveal your secrets to me." Eliyahu replied: "Now that you want to separate from me, I will explain everything to you and reveal the secrets of my actions. Know that the man whose cow I killed, his wife was to die the same day by divine decree, so I prayed to the Lord that his cow would die in place of his wife. In addition, I found that she was an excellent wife in all areas, and they will soon prosper.

The rich man for whom I built the wall, if I had let him do it on his own, he would have found in the foundations a great treasure of gold and silver. So I built it myself, but the wall has to collapse again and he won't rebuild it. Those for whom I prayed that they will all become leaders, is actually a curse. They will only have controversies. Every place where there are several leaders, the outcome will be a disaster. Those to whom I wished to have a single chief is a blessing. Peace will reign amongst them, they will succeed whatever they undertake, because they will follow only one advice. A famous proverb says that two captains sink a ship. Also, a city will be successful with a single leader.

Before I leave you, I'm going to teach you some principles that will help you. If you see a *rasha* (a wicked person) who succeeds in everything he does, let your inclination not drag you and do not be surprised, because this is for his ultmost misfortune. If you see a *tzadik* (a righteous) who suffers all his life, in hunger and thirst, lacking everything, or suffering a lot, do not be afraid or confused. Let not your inclination deceive you, nor should you have the slightest thought of suspicion about your Creator, who is Righteous, whose Decisions are just, for *Hashem* has his eyes fixed on the ways of man. Who would dare say to Him, "What are You doing?" They wished well to each other and Eliyahu continued on his way."

The verse says (Tehillim 115-4): *Their idols are silver and gold,* עֲצַבֵּיהֶם כֶּסֶף וְזָהָב. Idols are called עצבים, sadness is also עצב. Both words have the same root. Sadness comes when you forget *Hashem*, you think you have no hope. Everyone who is connected to *Hashem* is always happy, he knows that the Lord can change everything in an instant.

Smell is the sense that did not participate in Chava's sin with the serpent. "Ketores" (incense) is the main offering in divine service in the *Bais Hamikdosh.* Adam did not fault by smell. *Hashem* will never let man fall to the bottom of the precipice, He will always leave him an escape route, a rope to hang on to. With just one spark, you can start a big fire.

We need joy to serve *Hashem.* The Lord created the man "perfect" on one side (through studying the Torah, being merciful, etc.), and on the other side he is "lacking" (money, alcohol, gambling, etc.), he is weak. His weakness (each of us will identify it), it is the **main thing** that man must repair during his passage in this world.

All of us have a good and bad side. Realizing that we have a good side gives us joy, we are happy with all the good that we do. This joy gives us strength to correct what is negative in our personality. Life is Beautiful. It's a joy to live. Sadness, despair, depression, are a mistake. If we feel bad, it is because we lack sleep or that we feel empty and not full, in conclusion we are missing something. Without the night we wouldn't know the stars...

## *Divine Providence*

The Master of the world is omnipresent, the whole earth is full of his Glory!

*Boruch Hashem,* during my trips abroad, with the wish to spread the message of our masters, I have had the merit of contemplating how much *Hakodosh Boruch Hu* is by our side.

During a trip to Morocco, I prayed alone at Paris Orly airport at *Netz* time (sunrise) in the restricted area, because I could not pray with a *minyan* (a quorum of ten men). A man approached me and asked if I would lend him my *tefillin.* At the end of my *Tephilah,* I answered his request and he was able to pray. When we arrived at Casablanca airport, I offered him a book and he gave me his Parisian phone number. When I returned, I met him in his office, I offered him books, because he had many employees that I could approach in this way.

On the return from the same trip, we flew on a Boeing 737 with 3 seats on each side of the corridor. My seat was in the middle of one of the rows. *Boruch Hashem,* the passenger on my right was a man. I still didn't know who was going to sit on my left. For obvious reasons of *Tsnius* (modesty), it is best not to sit next to a woman. *Boruch Hashem,* a man wearing a cap, sat down on my left. I heard him book a taxi over the phone to meet him when he arrived. By saying his name to the booking agent, my doubt was confirmed. I was sitting with my *kippah,* he had not yet introduced himself. He was turning two clementines in his hand. He peeled one and brought it to his mouth, while discreetly pronouncing the blessing on the fruit of the tree. I replied just as discreetly "Amen". Special meals are usually served first. My host had given me a bag with sandwiches that I had eaten at the airport, I was not hungry. In my meal tray, there was an individually wrapped chocolate cookie, that's what I ate. When the light signals switched off, my neighbor got up and took a packet of the same cookies from his satchel. I then offered him to take advantage of my meal, he happily accepted. After the usual introductions, we spoke more than two hours of Torah, an unforgettable flight! When we arrived at Orly-south airport, he bought one of the last books I had left and offered to share his taxi.

After the unfortunate attack of the "Hypercacher" store in Paris, may *Hashem* avenge the blood of the victims, I went to Paris to distribute a new book. Rav Eliyahu *shlita* always welcomes me with great affection in his synagogue. I arrived there and found nine soldiers occupying the Rav's office. *Boruch Hashem,* my dear brother, found me accommodation for one week. The person who was to come and give me the keys lived in the suburbs of Paris and had to carry them to me by motorbike to the synagogue in the 11th arrondissement of Paris. At the agreed time, I receive a call on my cell phone to go out and pick up the keys. I then needed to go to the 18th arrondissement. To my surprise, my pleasant messenger arrived by car and accompanied me to the apartment, thus avoiding great fatigue. The other excellent news is that he later loaned me an apartment until the end of my Parisian stay, a pleasant loft five minutes walk from the synagogue where my books are kept, accompanying me again with his car to transfer from the 18th to the 11th arrondissement.

We say in the *Birkas Hamozon: "Blessed is the man that trusts in Hashem, then Hashem will be his security"* (Jeremiah 17-7).

Whoever wants to see *Hashem* will have no difficulty in contemplating His omnipresent Glory...

## *Yod: anovoh, humility*

Regarding *Moshe Rabbeinu,* the Torah reports (Bamidbar 12-3): *Now the man Moshe was very humble, above all men upon the face of the earth.* Rashi explains the word *humble* meaning **modest and patient.** The Ramban explains that *Hashem* reacted on behalf of Moshe (when Miriam spoke about him to Aaron) because of his great humility, knowing that he would not react to any argument or provocation, even knowingly.

The Talmud (Chulin 79a) reports that the world is maintained only by the merit of one who holds back at the time of a dispute, as the *Possuk* tells us (Job 26-7): *He suspends the earth over nothing.*

The "Proud" person thinks that everything he owns comes from his own strength, that everything is due to him. Real humility is knowing that everything that man has, does not come from him. *Moshe Rabbeinu* knew that he was on a unique level, that no one could reach. The Torah testifies that he spoke face-to-face with *Hakodosh Boruch Hu,* yet he said about himself and Aaron (Shemos 16-8): *and what are we?* Avraham said (Bereshis 18-27): *who am I but dust and ashes.* However with the dust (the earth) we accomplish the *mitzvah* of covering the blood of a slaughtered poultry, so actually it is a very useful material. King David said (Tehillim 22-7): *I am a worm.* This is a living creature (the *Midrash* says that David spoke like this because he was destined to die at birth and be eaten by worms, where it not for *Adam Harishon* who gave him 70 years of his life).

It is a fact, we must realize that what we have does not come from our own strength. This obligates us to use all that we have in order to be helpful to everyone, to act generously without pretext. This could be in a material sense as well as in the spiritual realm. A rich person will make others benefit from his money, not just his banker. An intelligent or wise person will benefit his neighbor from his advice and wisdom.

*Hakodosh Boruch Hu* gave us tools to use them wisely, as the Torah asks us (Devarim 12-28): *...that it may go well with you, and with your children after you for ever, when you do what is good and right in the eyes of the Lord your God.* Rashi explains: *"which is good,* in the eyes of Heaven. *Which is right,* in the eyes of man."

## *The Union of the Jewish People*

The Talmud (Taanis 17b) teaches us that the Sages decreed that we cannot fast from the beginning of the month of *Nissan* until the end of the feast of *Pesach* because of the two victories on the *Tsdukim* and *Baytosim* (Jews who reject the Oral Torah and only believe in the Written Torah).

When the Jewish People received the Torah on Mount Sinai, the *Midrash* says that *Hakodosh Boruch Hu* overturned the mountain and threatened the Nation to bury them alive if they did not receive the Torah. This threat only concerned the Oral Torah. The people had accepted the Written Torah and wanted to stop there. *Hakodosh Boruch Hu* wanted them to understand that the Written Torah is inseparable from the Oral Torah. Otherwise it is an open door to misunderstanding the verses, leading to misinterpretation and blatant transgression of the Torah, which in the end means spiritual or physical death of the individual, may *Hashem* preserve us from it.

The verse says (Vayikra 18-30): *Therefore you shall safeguard My charge,* literally "keep My guard". The Torah warns the Rabbinical Courts to enact rabbinical laws so as not to transgress prohibitions of the Torah, such as the flesh of chicken that cannot be eaten or cooked with milk (which is a rabbinical law), to avoid confusion and lead people to transgress the prohibition of the Torah of cooking the kid in its mother's milk (basar v'chalav).

Many verses of the Torah would be incomprehensible without the commentaries of our Elders *z'l.* The union of the Written Torah with the Oral Torah is the only way to understand the Torah in its true sense. Our master Moshe received the Oral Torah from the Mouth of the Almighty and transmitted it to us. This means that every commentary on the Oral Torah is from divine Source, transmitted from teacher to student since the gift of the Torah at Mount Sinai. There is no innovation of the Rabbis, may *Hashem* preserve us. The Torah ordered them to be the keepers of the Law in this world. In this case, the transgression of a rabbinical prohibition results in two prohibitions, one from the Torah and one from a rabbinic order.

These victories over the *Tsdukim* and the *Baytosim* that the Talmud recounts are so important that our Elders *z'l* instituted that this period would be prohibited from fasts and funeral orations *(hespedim).* These "reformists" wanted to harm the Jewish People by affecting their very essence, namely its unity, through the *Korban ha Tomid* (daily sacrifice offered in the morning and in the afternoon at the Temple of Jerusalem with Communal money). This sacrifice, due to its nature, united the Nation in their daily offering. A united Community seeking to serve *Hashem* together, as one. They misled the people that this sacrifice was an individual sacrifice and not a community sacrifice, in support of verses misinterpreted due to a lack of knowledge of the Oral Torah, this proves that these renegades wanted to damage the sacred union of the Jewish People. A victory in this direction proves the nonviability of the theses of “reformists” of all kinds. This is why this period has been decreed as so joyful.

### *Kei: shtikah, silence*

The "Chofetz Chayim" reports in his book "Shmiras ha Loshon" (Shaar ha Tevunah – 1st chapter) the following things:

The Talmud (Chulin 89a) deals with the question of Rav Yitschak, about the meaning of the verse (Tehillim 58-2): *Is there indeed silence* הַאֻמְנָם אֵלֶם *when you should be speaking righteousness? When you should be judging people with fairness?* What should be the אֻמָּנוּת "profession" of man in this world? Let him behave like a "mute", אִלֵּם. What the Torah designates as a profession is to teach us several points. First, it is obvious, a man who is not a craftsman, and wants to make a certain utensil, although he easily has in mind how to design it in all its forms, he will nevertheless find difficulty in achieving it in practice, because his hands are not accustomed to this. Unlike the craftsman who has had experience since his youth. This is so with the *Middah* (character trait) of silence. Anyone who has knowledge can imagine how precious this character trait is, because the person is protected through it from all the suffering that could be triggered by speech. In the absence of silence, he could suffer much anguish, as we will detail them later.

In any case, if a person decides to behave thus (to be silent) only when he is constrained by a *mitzvah* of the Torah, such as not to slander *(loshon hora),* to report *(rechilus),* to mock *mitzvos* and other kinds of forbidden words, yet apart from that he will speak whatever he wants, even words that are not necessary, (all the forbidden words described above) he will discover that he cannot avoid speaking maliciously since he is not accustomed to reducing his flow of words, as he has been used since his youth to say everything he thinks. However this is not the case if he becomes more and more accustomed to keeping silent, like the craftsman who practices his trade, to the point that being silent becomes natural for him and speaking freely without restraint becomes foreign to his personality, like a mute. The man can then be convinced that *Hashem* will prevent him from speaking forbidden words and behaving like a fool again.

*The Chofetz Chayim* adds that man must constantly keep in mind all his innumerable sins committed by speech so far, when in reality he should have been punished with mutism. Only because of divine Mercy has he been spared. **How could I still fail on this matter?**

The *Mishna* says (Avos 1-17): "Shimon his son (of Raban Gamliel) said: All my life I have grown up among the Wise, and I have found nothing more beneficial for the body than silence. The main thing is not in the study, but in the acts. And everyone who abounds in words leads to sin."

Rav Pinchas Kehati *z'l* in his commentary on this *Mishna* explains it in this way: "and I have found nothing more beneficial for the body than silence, quoting the Talmud (Pesachim 99b) which says that "silence is excellent for the Wise, all the more so for the fools", as the *Possuk* tells us

(Proverbs 17-28): *Even a fool will be considered wise if he his silent.* Rashi explains that one who abounds with words (even if he is wise) is considered a fool. It is also written (Proverbs 21-23): *One who guards his mouth and his tongue guards his soul from troubles.* Even if he is humiliated, he remains silent without answering.

The Talmud (Kidushin 71b) says: "Bavel's silence is his nobility. If you meet someone from Bavel who is silent and does not speak much, know that he comes from a good and noble family..."

The *Midrash Shmuel* explains that silence is beneficial even for the needs of the body, whereas it is not the case when it is a question of the needs of the *Neshama* (soul), in this case we are encouraged to expand our speech such as the study of Torah or *Tephilah* (prayer).

**And everyone who abounds in words leads to sin:** As the *Possuk* tells us (Proverbs 10-19) : *In a multitude of words offense will not be lacking; but he that restrains his lips is wise.* On this subject, the masters of the *Mussar* said: "Hold on to your tongue as you hold on to your money."

## *The joy of Rabbi Shimon ben Elazar*

The Talmud (Taanis 20a) reports an *Aggada* between Rabbi Shimon ben Elazar and *Eliyahu Hanavi:*

Our Masters have taught that a man should always be flexible like a reed and not hard (uncompromising) like an oak.

Rabbi Shimon ben Elazar was returning from *Migdal Gedor* (name of a city) from his master's house. He was riding his donkey and walking on the edge of the river. He was extremely happy and very proud of himself because he had studied a lot of Torah. He encountered a man (Rashi explains that it was *Eliyahu Hanavi* who came to lecture him on his behavior) who was ugly to the highest degree. This man greeted him by saying: "Shalom alecha Rabbi (peace be upon you, my master)". Rabbi Shimon did not return his salute but said to him: "Reyka (empty of everything)! How ugly you are! Are all the people in your city as ugly as you? He replied, "I don't know, but go to the Artisan who created me and tell Him how ugly the object He created is!"

Rabbi Shimon realized that he did wrong, got down from his donkey and bowed to the man saying: "I have said too much, forgive me!" "I will not forgive you until you go to the Artisan who created me by telling Him how ugly is the object He made!" Rabbi Shimon followed him to the city. The people of the city welcomed Rabbi Shimon with great honor: "Shalom alecha Rabbi Rabbi, Mori Mori". The man said to them, "Who is the person you name Rabbi Rabbi?" They answered him, "The one who follows you." "If he is a Rabbi, let there be no others like him in the People of Israel." They asked him his reason and he told them what happened. "Although he behaved like this with you, forgive him, he is a great scholar in Torah." He replied, "I forgive him in your honor, but he should not get accustomed to behaving like that."

Rabbi Shimon ben Elazar immediately went to the *Bais Hamidrash* (the house of studies) and taught: "Let man be as flexible as a reed and not hard as the oak. This is the reason why the reed merited to be used as a quill *(kulmus)* with which we write the *Sefer Torah, Tefillin* and *Mezuzos."*

## *Vav: mius betaanuguei haguf,* the revulsion of physical pleasures

The Torah commands us (Vayikra 19-2): *Ye shall be holy; for I the Lord your God am holy.* Rashi explains: "Stay away from forbidden relationships and sin, because wherever you find a barrier to debauchery, you find mention of holiness." "Ramban" explains (according to *Toras Kohanim)* that the Torah, in the simple sense, asks us to be ascetic[1] (abstain from allowed things). Another verse reports (Vayikra 20-7): *Sanctify yourselves therefore, and you will be holy; for I am the Lord your God;* as I am Holy, in the same way you will be holy. As I am Ascetic, in the same way you will be ascetic.

The reason the Torah warned us about forbidden relationships and forbidden foods, and allowed intimate relationships between man and his wife and the consumption of meat and wine, is that a man full of desire could spend his time with his wife or his many wives, make big feasts, say as many vulgarities as he wants, which the Torah has not explicitly prohibited, he will be then considered to be "contemptible" with approval from the Torah. This is why the Torah, after having completely forbidden prohibited relationships, wants us to distance ourselves from permitted things in general, such as limiting ourselves in intimate relationships, as is taught in

1 Ascetic: a person who, through asceticism, tends towards spiritual perfection.
Asceticism: discipline, set of exercises, behaviors, to which a person is bound for his spiritual improvement.

the Talmud (Berachos 22a): "Let Torah scholars not be present with their wives like roosters, but have intimate relationships according to the needs of the *mitzvah.*" Sanctify yourself by drinking as little wine as possible, such as the *Nazir* (who made the vow for a while not to consume wine or grape derivatives) which qualifies us as Holy (Bamidbar 6-5). We will also remember what was the consequence of the abuse of wine to Noah (who was mutilated by one of his sons when he was drunk) and to Lot (who had intimate relations with his daughters during his intoxication)... We must also be careful not to pronounce vulgar words, as the *Possuk* tells us (Isaiah 9-16): *for every one is ungodly and an evil-doer, and every mouth utters depravity...* We must sanctify ourselves with all the above to the point of reaching a high level of asceticism, as was reported about Rabbi Chiya, who never said a useless word during his existence.

*Ramban* goes on to remind us that sanctifying oneself reminds us of the ablution of the hands before a meal *(netilas yodayim);* to be holy is to wash your hands after a meal *(mayim acharonim).*

We also need to get away from the many people who spiritually deteriorate by abusing permitted things. The role of man is to raise our material world to *Hakodosh Boruch Hu,* so that He can reside there and divine Providence is revealed here below. The more man benefits from this world, the closer he gets to the earth, the more he moves away from *Hashem.* These are pleasures that are outside the scope of *mitzvos,* unlike *Shabbos,* holidays and meals in honor of a *mitzvah.*

The Talmud (Kesubos 104a) tells us about the final moments of Rabbi Yehuda ha Nassi: "At the time of Rebbi's death, he raised his ten fingers to the sky and said: "Master of the world, it is known and revealed before You that I have toiled (throughout my life) with my ten fingers in Torah study and that I have not benefited (from this world) even with my little finger. May it be Your will that there shall be peace in my resting place." Immediately, a heavenly Voice was heard: "Let him enter in peace, rest on his couch, the one who follows His straight path."

The Talmud comes to teach us that Rebbi did not take advantage of this world for his own pleasure or honor, although he was very wealthy and the greatest Sage of his generation. All of his reward came only from the application of *mitzvos.* Indeed, he got married, had children, ate well on *Shabbos,* on *Yomim Tovim,* at a *bris-milah,* a *bar-mitzvah* or a wedding, but the bare minimum was enough for the days of the week.

The highest level for humans is to revel in *Hashem.* Whoever delights in this world only for himself is considered to be using the strength of the delight of *Hashem,* which is contrary to our purpose in this world, namely to bring closer and allow divine Providence to reside on earth. We will understand why the Israeli expression "get a kiff" has no place in Judaism, except in the context of a *mitzvah,* in the correct measure and fashion.

In conclusion, we understand the reason why a physical pleasure becomes "repugnant", when it takes us away from our essential duty to serve the Master of the world.

## *In a permitted manner*

The Talmud (Menachos 44a) tells us of a wonderful story about the *mitzvah* of *Tsitsis:*

A man was meticulous in correctly fulfilling the *mitzvah* of *Tsitsis* [1]. He once heard that there was a courtesan across the seas asking for her services four hundred *zehuvim*. He sent her this fortune and set a date for their interview. When the time came, he appeared at her door and the woman's servant brought him in. She put in place seven beds one on top of the other, six in silver linked each by a silver ladder, and the seventh in gold linked by a gold ladder. The courtesan went up to the golden bed, stretched out naked on the bed. He climbed in turn all the beds and also lay down naked next to her. His four *Tsitsis* came to hit him in the face. He climbed down immediately and sat on the floor. She did the same and asked him, "I swear I will not let you go if you don't tell me the flaw you saw in me". He replied, "I swear I have never seen a woman as beautiful as you. However, I am a Jew and the Lord has commanded us with a *mitzvah* called *Tsitsis.* It is written twice: *I am the Lord your God;* I am the One who will make the wrongdoer pay his due and I am the One who will pay the reward. The *Tsitsis* appeared as four witnesses, that is the reason for my abandonment". She said to him: "I will not let you go until you tell me your name, the name of your city, the name of your Rabbi and the name of the *Bais Hamidrash* where you learn Torah.

1 *Tsitsis:* fringes that are attached to the corners of four-cornered garments worn by men.

He wrote her everything on a piece of paper, put it in her hands and took leave. She was very impressed with this man's self-control and the miracle that had happened. Subsequently, she sold all of her goods. She gave a third to the authorities (in order to let her convert and leave "her function"), donated a third to the poor and kept for herself a third and the seven beds.

She went to Rabbi Chiya's *Bais Hamidrash* and said to him, "Rabbi! Order that I be converted." He replied: "My daughter! Would you have placed your eyes on one of my students? She handed him the paper she had in her possession and told him the whole story. Rabbi Chiya said to her, "Go and take possession of what is due to you." After her conversion (and their marriage), the beds that were once forbidden, were now permitted.

So was the reward of this man in this world for having restrained himself from sin, oh how will it be in the future world!

The "Sefer Abudraham" teaches us the importance of the *mitzvah* of *Tsitsis:*

The *mitzvah* of *Tsitsis* is great enough to be equivalent to all the *mitzvos* of the Torah (Menachos 43b), as the *Possuk* tells us (Bamidbar 15-39): *the sight of which will remind you of all the mitzvos of Hashem.* In Hebrew, the numerical value of this verse corresponds to 612. By adding the *mitzvah* of the *Tsitsis,* we get 613, which is the number of all the mitzvos of the Torah. The numerical value of the word *Tsitsis* in Hebrew written with two "Yod", צִיצִית, is 600. By adding the eight threads and the five knots which form the *Tsitsis,* we arrive at the count of 613. In the Torah, the word *Tsitsis* is written with a single letter *Yod,* י. The "Midrash Tanchuma" explains that the word *Tsitsis* is written three times in the Torah. However, it is written once לְצִיצִת, with the letter "Lamed", which has the numerical value thirty. We thus found the account of the three missing *Yods.*

On the four corners of a cloth attached with *Tsitsis,* there are thirty-two threads which are doubled, totaling sixty-four. This corresponds to the 64 faces which are represented on the divine Throne, also as the *Possuk* tells us (Ezekiel 10-14): *And every one had four faces...* You will find 64 words from the beginning of the verse (Bamidbar 15-38/41) דַּבֵּר אֶל-בְּנֵי יִשְׂרָאֵל until אֲנִי ה' אֱלֹהֵיכֶם, in order to remind us, so to speak, that the divine Presence is in front of the one who performs this *mitzvah.* It is written in the *Sifri* and the *Talmud Yerushalmi* that anyone who performs the *mitzvah* of *Tsitsis* is considered as if he has received the divine Presence (end of quote).

According to these teachings, we will do our utmost and will no longer hesitate to wear under our clothes all day long a "Talis Koton" in order to perform this important *mitzvah,* which costs only a few dollars. A woolen *Talis Koton* is, according to all *Poskim,* a *Torah mitzvah,* while a cotton *Talis,* according to some *Poskim,* is rabbinical. The *Pele Yoetz* said he looks like someone who could win a thousand gold coins and accepts only five hundred. For those who pretend that they are hot with a woolen *Talis Koton,* it will be enough to wear it on a cotton T-shirt. Some are accustomed to hanging the strings outside their clothes, while others keep them inside. Everyone should question his Rabbi on which option to take. Rabbi David Pinto *shlita* taught us regarding the one who applies the *mitzvah* of the *Tsitsis,* we consider him as if he has on him a "mitzvah counter" which runs continuously. The *Vilna Gaon* started to cry as he left this world. He explained to his students that for a small sum in this world, we can observe a *mitzvah* which is equivalent to all those of the Torah, whilst in the future world, this is no longer possible...

## *Kei: simcha tmidis bechelko,* to be constantly happy with his portion

The *Mishna* (Avos 4-1) says, "Who is (truly) rich?" One who is happy with his portion, as the *Possuk* tells us (Tehillim 128-2): *When you eat the labor of your hands, praiseworthy shall you be, and it shall be well with you.* ***Praiseworthy shall you be,*** refers to this world. ***It shall be well with you,*** is reserved for you in the world to come.

Rabbi Ovadia Yossef *zt'l* in his book "Anaf Etz Avot" (page 231) brings on this subject a marvelous story of the "Naggid", Rabbeinu David, the grandson of the *Rambam,* from his book "Midrash David":

This is the story of a poor man who earned enough to support his family. He was always happy with what *Hakodosh Boruch Hu* gave him, little or much. Each evening after the family dinner, everyone praised *Hashem* for all the good received. The family would then sit, one of the children would play the violin, another would sing, play the tambourine and they would party and dance, for an hour or two, then go to bed.

One evening, the king passed by their door and listened to the music without disturbing them. He came back to listen to them three nights in a row. The king summoned the poor man to the palace and asked him, "How much money do you have?" "Your Majesty, I am a poor man, I have no money, only what I earn on a daily basis, and with that I feed my family. I rejoice in what the Creator, blessed be He, gives me even if it is not much, and I dance and sing with my family every evening." The king thought to himself that if in such a situation of poverty, they rejoice and praise the Lord, blessed be He, oh how much more their joy and praises towards *Hashem,* blessed be He, would increase tenfold if they get rich. The king ordered his servants to cover him with gold!

Our man took the gold and went to his house. He put the coins in a box and noticed that it was not full to the brim, there was a little missing. He agreed with his wife to work until the box filled completely. The poor man became worried and anxious. He put everything he earned into the box every day without it filling up. The family stopped singing and dancing every night, worries and anxiety now dominated them.

After a while, the king walked past their door. He found them asleep, without any expression of joy. He returned two then three times, without hearing their voices. The king summoned the poor man and asked him, "How are you?" "Oh your majesty! When I had no money I was happy, I didn't need any money. Now, worries dominate me, I persist in wanting to fill the box, which is not filling." With that the king took back all the money. The poor man returned to his original life style, resuming his dancing and singing.

*Rabbi Ovadia mi Bartenura* comments: "Who is (genuinely) rich? Who is able to praise his wealth? He who is happy with his lot." Only one who is happy with the portion he has received can be considered as a real rich man, without ever complaining, and who praises *Hashem* for all the good and fortune (in a positive or negative sense), unlike those who have a lot of wealth and want more, or who have little and want more.

According to the *Ramchal,* this also concerns the spiritual realm. For example: a person has the ability to study Torah well for one hour, while their friend manages to study for three hours. He is happy with what he has managed to study, without being disappointed that he has not done more. On the Day of Judgment, he will not be reproached for not having used the capacities that *Hashem* gave him well. However, an individual who has not fully exploited his spiritual capacities will have to account for them.

*Tiferet Israel* explains that if a man works to eat and not to get rich, then he will be happy, the good will be his share. He goes on to say that he is happy in this world and will receive the good reserved for the future world, for he is the one who suffices with a little. When man is joyful and satisfied, he is in a position to be happy in this world, furthermore the good will be reserved for him in the future world thanks to this, because by the mere fact of being satisfied with a little, he will not infringe upon the sin of not coveting, he will not steal, will not cheat, and does not infringe any prohibition of the Torah to earn more, because he fears the punishment of the future world.

The last of the Ten Commandments is (Shemos 20-13): (לֹא תַחְמֹד) *You shalt* ***not covet*** *your neighbor's house; you shalt not covet your neighbor's wife, nor his man-servant, nor his maid-servant, nor his ox, nor his ass, nor any thing that is your neighbor's.*

The *Kli Yakar* explains to us that the location on the *Luchos* of the *mitzvah* of not coveting (10th position) and that of honoring one's parents (5th position), both are at the bottom of the Law Tables, one opposite on the other: *Mechilta* explains that everyone who covets will come to bear a son who will curse him. It's difficult to understand, what is the relationship between these two commandments? It seems that everyone who covets the wife of his neighbor surely thinks of her when he has an intimate relationship with his own wife. It is as if the son of this union was born to the woman he coveted, which is why he does not honor his real mother, since his father was thinking of another woman during that moment. This son also does not honor his father, because he who covets the wife of others does not intend to father children, it is only to satisfy his *Taavos* (seeking pleasure). As everything goes according to *Kavanah* (intention), this child will not honor his father since he had no intention of having a son.

The lust for money is also attached to the *mitzvah* of honoring one's parents, because one who covets the money of his neighbors cannot honor them, since he has a burning desire to monopolize their wealth. Honoring your parents also has ramifications on your money, because you sometimes have to feed them, dress them, etc. There is no doubt that this man will not be generous with their needs and will not care for them in sufficient quantities.

## *Rabbi Yochanan or Ilfa?*

The Talmud (Taanis 21a) tells us the following story:

Ilfa[1] (name of a great Sage) and Rabbi Yochanan were studying Torah together. Their incomes had become so meager that they became poverty stricken. They said to themselves: "Let us get up and go make some money, so that we can live and apply the verse (Devarim 15-4): *However there may be no needy among you* (in order to not need others).

They headed towards the market place. They stopped on the way under a dilapidated wall to eat bread. Then came two servicing angels. Rabbi Yochanan heard one of them say, "let us collapse this wall to kill them, since they have put aside the life of the future world (the study of Torah) to deal with worldly affairs (trade for income)." The second angel said to the other, "let us leave them alive, because one of them will become a great personality." Rabbi Yochanan had heard the discussion between the two angels, but not Ilfa. Rabbi Yochanan asked his friend: "Did you hear something?" He replied in the negative[2]. Rabbi

1 Ilfa was cited first because he was greater in Torah than Rabbi Yochanan (according to Rashi).

2 "Ben Yehoyada" explains that since Rabbi Yochanan asked Ilfa if he had heard anything, Ilfa obviously understood that Rabbi Yochanan had heard something. The reason why Ilfa did not ask him anything is in the rest of the verse, *that there will always be needy people in the country.* Ilfa thought that Heaven did not want Rabbi Yochanan to succeed in trade, while he had all his chances.

Yochanan said to himself that since he was the only one who had heard the conversation between the two angels, he presumed it was him the angel referred to about becoming the great personality. Rabbi Yochanan decided to return to the *Yeshiva* to study Torah, and to apply the verse (Devarim 15-11): *Now there will always be needy people in the land* [3]. Rabbi Yochanan returned, and not Ilfa.

When Ilfa returned from his business (after a short period), Rabbi Yochanan had been appointed *Rosh (director of) Yeshiva* [4]. People said to Ilfa, "if you had stayed studying Torah, we would have chosen you as *Rosh Yeshiva."* Hearing this, Ilfa climbed the mast of a boat and said: "If one of you asks me a question about a *Baraisa* of Rabbi Chiya and Rabbi Oshaya, and if I do not give you the source in the *Mishna,* I would throw myself down and

3 "Ben Yehoyada" explains that Rabbi Yochanan did not say anything to Ilfa, because he knew that he should have been named *Rosh Yeshiva* in his place, since he was greater than him in Torah. And as Rabbi Yochanan was obviously to be named *Rosh Yeshiva,* according to the discussion between the angels, he did not want Ilfa to die, since the revelations of the second angel were to come true.

4 Rashi explains that the habit at the time was to enrich the *Rosh Yeshiva,* as we learn from *Kohen Gadol* (Vayikra 21-10): *As for the Kohen superior to his brothers.* Higher in wealth. We understand from this how much Rabbi Yochanan has gained from returning to the *Yeshiva.* He did not fear his position of poverty, because he knew that his luck could turn at any moment, like a poor man who sometimes has plenty and sometimes, that *Hashem* preserves us, lacks everything.

drown (because although I was trading, I studied more than Rabbi Yochanan and I did not forget my study)."

## *The sacred union*

*Hakodosh Boruch Hu* communicates with us by transmitting His messages from our holy Torah, written or oral. *Boruch Hashem,* for thousands of years, the message has succeeded and the communication has never been interrupted, *on You Hashem we depend and we hang on Your goodwill!* Nowadays, the ultimate communication tool is the smartphone. In record time, people hardly talk to each other but send short messages, thumbs replacing lips. In many families, SMS has become the most common means of communication. "Orthodox" mothers walk their children with their *kosher phones* stuck between their headscarves and their ears. Babies are no longer entitled to sweet words and tokens of affection during their walk. Mom is busy with her many "contacts". In all movements of current Judaism, everyone has their own communication tool which never leaves their side. Couples in the restaurant pay all their attention to the screen of their iPhone, and not the spouse! Others spend the meal showing their latest vacation or travel videos, if not an exceptional report! We only see or watch, we transmit streams of messages without being a real communicator, we are rather virtual... Voyeurism is king in the blind kingdom...

The book of *Devarim* only asks us to practice the Torah, to speak about it, to teach it, to study it, to transmit it to our children and to our students. In conclusion, may our holy Torah be the essential of our life. This can only be transmitted through a real and human communication, not virtual and inhuman. The iPhone has become the greatest anti-communication tool of all time. Its ravages can no longer be counted because they are so numerous. Man has become a slave to the machine and its mind-numbing applications. We have the impression of having to deal with a tornado which engulfs everything in its path, but we have no right to be silent, it would be to be an accomplice of the disaster of an entire generation and, God forbid, following.

The advantage of the iPhone is that it obeys the finger and the eye, without ever asking for anything in return. It answers everything. While a wife or her husband does not have this “advantage”!

The cement of a couple is their bond, their sacred union! A communicating couple is a living couple. The fiber of life is the exchange of simple words, spoken words that will be heard and listened to. It's everyone's expectation, a vital need, like eating and drinking. Having the finesse of heart to undertake projects in common, without involving either the children or the entourage, is the best agreement. For example, studying a *Mussar* book together, growing small sweet peppers together in a pot to harvest the salad of affection, allows you to share very significant moments. Everyone will choose what will suit them best, while favoring an activity where no one else is involved. Life goes by so quickly, the birth of children, their education, their joys, it does not leave time for the couple to have sufficient quality time to be sufficiently united when the house is empty as and when time allows, in order not to find yourself later wondering who is that stranger in front of you! May *Hashem* preserve us from it. King Solomon has already said (Koheles 4-12): *but a triple bond (a thread made up of several threads) is even less easy to break.* Each act that the couple perform together will be a new thread woven between them, in order to strengthen their bond to become tear-proof over time.

**The oxygen of a woman** (according to Rabbanit Sima Batsri *z'l* book "Marriage? A challenge!") **is her husband's compliments, little touches and affection in everyday life.** What gives her the strength to continue to take care of all the repetitive tasks of the home is to have the feeling of being appreciated by her husband for all the good done to their family. While what gives man the energy to continue, in his pursuit is the feeling of succeeding in what he undertakes. The *Pele Yoetz* teaches us that the greatest pleasure for man is earning money, it is the culmination of all his efforts. The woman is more sentimental, being appreciated is her height of happiness, that helps and stimulates her to also improve in all areas. In this regard, our Sages *z'l* taught us that the Egyptians, during the servitude of the children of Israel in Egypt, compelled men to do the tasks of women, and women to do the work of men. It is easy to understand that a woman does not have the physique to carry heavy stones. However, why is it so hard for a man to do household chores? Man has the nature of doing things that last a long time, like building a house, roads, etc. Whenever he sees his achievement, he derives personal satisfaction from it. On the other hand, the woman often does "ephemeral things", such as a good cake that ends in five minutes or a wonderful dish that did not stay long in the pot (although it took her several hours to prepare them). In this case, what remains for our lovely wife for all her efforts to please us? **Our compliments!** It is the indelible mark of the expression of our gratitude towards her kindness towards us (words gathered according to a conversation with Rav Gabriel Lemel *shlita).* An intelligent husband will be **generous in compliments** addressed to his wife and **miserly in reproaches.** In addition, it will be a wonderful example for the education of their children.

Our Sages *z'l,* in the first *Mishna* of the *Kidushin* treaty, teach us that we can marry a woman with only one *Pruta* (coin worth roughly five cents that we give her in front of two *kosher* witnesses) or by **the value of a *Pruta.*** How much does a compliment cost? **Nothing!** But it makes her so happy! Our Sages *z'l* showed us the way thousands of years ago. Whoever does this, acquires[1] his wife daily, as if they were getting married every day! Some men imagine that complimenting them will obligate them much more towards their wives. This is not true, it will simply make her happier and more considerate of her husband. This is the principle of a symbiotic relationship. About this principle, the word "couple" in Hebrew is written: **זוג** – *Zug, Zayin–Vav–Gimmel.* The letters *Zayin* and *Gimmel* are actually the same letter but reversed, they represent

1 To acquire his wife according to the Torah, to do *Kinyan* with his wife, is to do an act which prohibits her from the whole world and allows her only to her husband. Not as some people might think, "buy her", *Hashem* save us.

the man and the woman. In the middle, the letter *Vav* makes the link between the two, it is the "Vav hachibur", that is to say '*Hashem*' according to Kabbalah. It's the Master of the world who makes the link between man and woman. The "Ramak", may his merit protect us, in his book "Tomer Dvora", teaches us that *Hashem* rules the world according to thirteen *Middos* (principles) of mercy. In order to be like Him, we must behave in His image, yet not being reliant on image alone without actions. We can also note that the letters *Zayin* and *Gimmel* each have a rounded shape, like a utensil ready to contain what we will pour into it. *Hashem* established as a condition for the creation of the world to give without expecting to receive anything in return from anyone. A husband and wife must be constantly in the position of giving to their spouse without expecting anything in return. It is the satisfaction of giving that makes us happy, like our patriarch Avraham, who gave without limit and only got richer. His nephew Lot, unwilling to "squander" all of his possessions, separated from his uncle to go and live in Sodom, where charity was punishable by death. His end was to lose all his possessions, some of his children, his wife and to have fathered with his own daughters... When we are waiting to receive, we are always disappointed. By giving, we are always happy!

The *Maharsha* wrote about the Talmud *Kesubos* 8a: "At the beginning, *Hakodosh Boruch Hu* wanted to edify creation by the attribute of justice and found that it could not be maintained, etc. The same is true for the creation of man and woman. At first, *Hashem* wanted to make two creatures, like all other creatures. However, when He saw that the man was fundamentally quarrelsome, that the world could not be maintained without peace, without *Shalom, Hashem* put his Name, יה, between man, איש, and the woman, אשה. *Hashem* then created a single creature, just like his Name which is unique in His world, maybe there will be *Shalom* between them, as if they were one body." If we remove the *Yod* from the man or the *Hey* from the woman, they only have the *Alef* and the *Shin, Esh,* אש, fire in Hebrew! A couple can only live in harmony if the Name of *Hashem* creates the link between them. If one or both of them discard their part of the divine Name, the fire of dispute is declared. The cement of the Jewish home, of a couple worthy of the Name, can only be so in the application of our holy Torah. A couple who imagine that they have succeeded their lives together without respecting the divine rules live in illusion.

Since their creation, man and woman, by the essence of their name, have been attached to the divine Name. To detach oneself from the divine Name is to detach oneself from our Source of life. A relationship can only flourish and especially be sustained when applying the rules decreed by our Creator, in His honor, not for our own interest, and especially not according to the rules of the liberal and depraved society that surround us, may *Hashem* preserve us from it, *Amen!*

If we behave with our wives and our husbands as *Hashem* behaves with us, the doors of happiness will open wide.

Endure, be patient endlessly, forgive, ignore the faults of the other, be affectionate without getting angry, be kind to each other, never hold a grudge, remember only the good received, stifle evil, have mercy, be indulgent without being picky about anything, in no case humiliate (according to our master Rabbi Eliezer Papo *zt'l,* be humiliated without ever being the one who humiliates) in short, walk in the ways of *Hakodosh Boruch Hu.*

## *Shalom*

The "Sefer Abudraham" explains to us why the word "Shalom" is placed at the end of the *Kaddish.* Through his teaching, we will realize why it is the only utensil that can contain the *"Brocha",* the blessing, and how it is fundamental in all areas:

The reason why *Shalom* is placed at the end of the *Kaddish* is because it is equivalent to everything. It is written in the "Yoitser": "Who makes Shalom and creates everything." It is taught in "Toras Kohanim": Perhaps you will say to yourself: "Here is food, here is drink, if there is no peace (Shalom), there is nothing!" We are taught (Vayikra 26-6): *I will make peace prevail in this country...* We deduce that Shalom is equivalent to everything.

"Great is Shalom" (Chulin 141a), because *Hakodosh Boruch Hu* made it permissible to erase his Great Name written in holiness to establish *Shalom* between a husband and his wife.

Great is *Shalom,* because it glorifies the Torah in peace, as the *Possuk* tells us (Proverbs 3-17): *and all her paths are peaceful (Shalom).*

Great is *Shalom,* because although in the heavens there is neither jealousy nor hatred nor an evil eye between the angels, despite everything they need *Shalom,* as the *Possuk* tells us (Job 25-2): *He makes peace (Shalom) in His high places.*

To return to the *Shalom* between a husband and his wife, the "Sefer Abudraham" explains to us the reason why women are dispensed from *mitzvos Asseh* (positive commandments which are realized by an action) which are linked to time:

We learn from the Talmud (Kidushin 34a) that women are exempt from *mitzvos Asseh* which are linked to time, by the juxtaposition of the verse of the *mitzvah of Tefillin* and that of the teaching of the Torah (Devarim 4-9): *make them known unto your sons,* (we deduce) and not to your daughters. The reason why women are exempt from time-related *mitzvos Asseh* is because the wife is subject to her husband in order to take care of all his material needs. If she had the obligation to adhere to the time-related *mitzvos Asseh,* it is possible that the moment she would perform this *mitzvah,* her husband would ask her to carry out a task for him, and if she would be occupied in carrying out the command of her Creator and put aside that of her husband, look out for her husband! If she prioritizes what her husband demands and would put aside the order of her Creator, woe to her from her Creator! This is the reason why the Creator dispensed her, so that *Shalom* reigns between her and her husband (end of quote).

## *Rambam*

Our master the *Rambam,* may his merit protect us, teaches us and summarizes in four *Halachos* all the rules to be applied during marital life (Nashim, Hilchos Ishus 15, laws 17 to 20), whether for the husband or his wife, so as to achieve perfect harmony in the couple, with the help of the One who makes *Shalom* in the world, *Hakodosh Boruch Hu!*

17. Each man has the obligation to admonish his wife (note: in the sense of warning her about certain behaviors, take her back and indicate the paths to follow, while reminding her that she is only allowed to him). Our Sages have said that a man does not admonish his wife unless an air of purity[1] has entered him. He will not admonish her to excess. He will not rape her and will not have a forced intimate relationship, but only with her consent, by speaking to her[2] and with joy.

18. Our Sages thus ordered the woman to be modest inside her house and that she should not joke too much nor be too frivolous with her husband. That she does not formally demand of her husband to have an intimate relationship and that she does not talk about this subject[3]. That she does not deny herself to her husband to make

1 Rashi in the Sotah treaty (3a) explains: "An air of purity: that he hates *Pritsus* (vulgarity)."

2 Before and not during the act, which is strictly prohibited.

3 However, suggestive behavior is permitted.

him suffer so that he loves her more, but she will oblige him at every moment that he wishes[4]. Let her be vigilant with his close family and the people in her house so that he does not suspect her. Let the wife move away from scandalous situations and from what looks like scandal.

19. Our Sages thus commanded man to honor his wife more than himself and to love her as himself. If he has the means, he will be generous to her according to his resources. Let him not be too harsh towards her (note: so as not to arrive at the situation that she fears him to excess) and let him speak to her calmly; he will not be sad or irritated.

20. Our Sages thus ordered the woman to honor her husband to the highest point, to fear him and that all her actions be according to his directives. In her eyes, he will be like a governor or a king. She will act according to the wishes of his heart and will drive away everything he hates.

This is how the holy and pure sons and daughters of Israel behave as a couple. And according to these paths (note: behaviors), their life will be pleasant and worthy of praise.

4 As far as the husband is available to his wife for privacy, so is the wife according to many opinions.

### *King David*

The Talmud (Sanhedrin 22a) reports the episode of King David with his servant Avishag (Kings 1-1): *Now King David was old and stricken in years; and they covered him with clothes, but he could get no heat.* No clothes or blankets were enough to warm his body.

Rashi explains : **"But he could get no heat":** our masters said (Berachos 62b) that anyone who behaves disdainfully towards clothes (because he tore the corner of King Shaul's coat), ultimately he will not benefit. *Midrash Aggada* reports the words of Rabbi Shmuel bar Nachmani: "When David saw the angel standing over Jerusalem with a sword in his hand, in fear, his blood became cold."

Verse 2: *His servants said to him: "Let there be sought for my lord the King a young virgin; and let her stand before the King, and be a companion unto him; and let her lie in your bosom, that my lord the King may get heat."*

Rashi explains: "**Virgin**: the blood of virginity heats her flesh."

Verse 3: *So they sought for a beautiful girl throughout all the borders of Israel, and they found Avishag the Shunammite, and brought her to the King.*

Verse 4: *And the girl was very beautiful; and she became a companion to the King, and she served him; but the King knew her not.*

Rashi explains: "**But the King knew her not:** a virgin woman has a much warmer body than a deflowered woman; our masters said (Sanhedrin 22a): because of the verse (Devarim 17-17) *He must not have many women either,* he already had eighteen wives. Which is the limit allowed for a king according to the Torah."

"Metsudas David" explains that the blood of a young virgin woman heats her body to the highest level. Avishag's beauty proved the abundance of her blood, which created excess heat in her body. The "Mahari" explains that it was enough for her to be close to King David and, by the simple fact of looking at her, it warmed his body. A deflowered woman loses two things: part of her beauty and the extra heat from the presence in her body of the blood of virginity. The Talmud (Kesubos) explains to us that virginity is not only the hymen, a simple skin, but like a pocket of blood present in the intimacy of the woman.

To isolate oneself with a single woman is a rabbinical prohibition. Since King David was in medical danger, for this reason the Sages allowed him to be alone with Avishag. The Talmud (Sanhedrin 22a) reports that Avishag asked King David to marry her. He replied that he had no right to divorce or repudiate one of his eighteen wives or concubines without good reason to take her as a wife. Avishag did not accept this pretext and replied to the King that he refused because he no longer had the strength to be with a woman, given his advanced age. To prove her wrong, the Talmud reports that King David had thirteen relationships with one of his favorite wives, Batsheva. "Ben Yehoyada" explains that King David made a great *Tikun (Yichudim)* by bringing abundance to the earth from "the thirteen attributes of mercy of Hashem". This will help us understand the level of holiness that can be achieved during an intimate act. Our Sages didn't name a couple's room "the Holy of Holies" for nothing! Intimacy is seen by the Torah as a most beautiful act. It brings life to earth, a blessing and binds the couple who become one flesh, a thousand miles from a bestial act, in fact it is the cement of their affection. Several of our masters *z'l* have written prayers to be pronounced before the act, in order to ward off the "bad inclination" (because where there is physical pleasure, this evil is always present, according to our master Rabbi Eliezer Papo *zt'l)* and bring the divine Presence to us.

The Talmud continues: Rav Shemen bar Abba said: "Oh how difficult divorce is, to the point that our Sages allowed King David to isolate himself with a single woman so as not to divorce one of his wives or to repudiate one of his concubines." Rabbi Eliezer said that anyone who divorces his first wife, even the *Mizbeach* (the altar), sheds tears over him, as the *Possuk* tells us (Malachi 2-13): *And this is a second sin that you do: you cover the altar of the Lord with tears, with weeping, and with sighing, insomuch that He will no longer turn to your offering any more, neither receive it with good will from your hand.* Also (Malachi 2-14): *Yet you say: "Why is this?" Because the Lord has testified between you and the wife of your youth, against whom you have betrayed, though she is your companion, and the wife of your covenant.*

Rabbi Yochanan said that anyone who loses his first wife is considered to experience the destruction of the Temple during its existence, as the *Possuk* tells us (Ezekiel 24-16): *Son of man, behold, I take away from you the desire of your eyes in a plague; yet neither shalt you lament nor weep, neither shall your tears run down.* Also (Ezekiel 24-18): *So I spoke to the people in the morning, and in the evening my wife died.* Also (Ezekiel 24-21): *Behold, I will profane My sanctuary, the pride of your power, the desire of your eyes, and the longing of your soul.* Rabbi Alexandri said that anyone who loses his wife during his lifetime, his world is clouded[1], as the *Possuk* tells us (Job 18-6): *The light shall be dark in his tent, and his lamp over him shall be put out.*

Rashi explains: **"The light shall be dark in his tent:** regarding his tent, this is his wife." Rabbi Yossi Bar Chanina said that his steps are weakened, as the *Possuk* tells us (Job 18-7): *The steps of his strength shall be constrained.* Rabbi Abahu said he has no one left to advise him[2], according to the rest of the verse: *and his own*

1 The Talmud (Yevomos 63a) compares the wife to that which "lights up the sight" of her husband, because without her help he cannot maintain himself. For example, a man brings wheat to his wife, does he eat wheat grains? He brings her linen, does he dress in linen? Obviously not! It turns out that she brightens his eyesight and keeps him standing. By losing his wife, may *Hashem* preserve us from it, his world becomes obscured because he has lost the one who "lights up his sight" (Maharsha).

2 The Talmud (Baba Metsia 59a) recommends that a man accept his wife's advice regarding the smooth running of the house.

*counsel shall cast him down.* Raba Bar Bar Channah said on behalf of Rabbi Yochanan that uniting a man and a woman is as hard as splitting the *Yam Suf* (sea of rushes[3]), as the *Possuk* tells us (Tehillim 68-7): *God settles the solitary to dwell in a house; He releases the prisoners into prosperity.* However, Rav said in the name of Rabbi Yehuda, forty days before the conception of the child, a heavenly voice announces so and so to marry so and so. It is not difficult, because in this case it is the first *Zivug* (wife). In statement it refers to the second *Zivug,* Rav Shmuel Bar Nachman said that everything is replaceable, except for the wife of his youth, as the *Possuk* tells us (Isaiah 54-6): *and a wife of youth, can she be rejected?* Rav Yehuda taught his son Rav Yitschak that a man is only satisfied by his first wife[4], as the *Possuk* tells us (Proverbs 5-18): *Your source will be blessed; and you will rejoice with the wife of your youth.* "Like who?" Asked Rav Yitschak. "Like your mother!" Answered Rav Yehuda. "Yet

---

Without his wife, it is difficult for him to manage his home (Ben Yehoyada).

3 To split the sea in two when leaving Egypt (in twelve according to some opinions), *Hashem* changed the rules of nature. In comparison, a couple must adapt to each other to bond. **This forces us to change or correct our nature, a daily job requiring a lot of effort.**

4 "Ben Yehoyada" explains that the husband freely confides in his first wife, which is why she knows exactly how to behave with him to fulfill all his wishes. In the case of a second wife, the husband is ashamed to disclose everything to her, which is why she cannot satisfy him properly.

you brought me the verse one day (Ecclesiastes 7-26): *and I find more bitter than death the woman, whose heart is snares and nets, and her hands are chains;* I asked you like who? You replied: like your mother who is a rough woman. However, she is not spiteful." Rav Shmuel Bar Unya said on behalf of Rav that a woman can only bind a covenant with the one who made her (a *Keli,* a utensil) capable of procreating, as the *Possuk* tells us (Isaiah 54-5): *For your Maker is your husband, the Lord of hosts is His name;* (We will understand the importance of marrying a virgin woman.)

In view of all these teachings of our Holy Torah, we draw the conclusion to which point we must do everything or support everything for a good understanding with the woman of our youth. **To imagine that the solution lies with another woman is a pure illusion...**

### *A just-in-time factory*

In industry, just-in-time is a production method to keep stock to a minimum. However, a defect or a delay in delivery from a supplier quickly leads to a drop in production rate, or even a halt in production. It is a fairly stressful method, since it is dependent on factors external to the plant.

Our very dear wives have many "traits in common" with this kind of management.

A man has possibilities, he can dispense or act within his means, no more.

A woman has needs, she is in a constant dynamic position, managing events in a tense flow.

She must prepare and send the children to school on time with their snacks, prepare her husband's breakfast, who returns at a specific time from the synagogue. Thereafter, she does the housework, laundry, sewing, shopping, etc. At noon, she prepares a meal for her children. Sometimes her husband comes home for lunch and he may be ravenous... At 4:30 pm., the kids come back from school and she must feed them again. Her husband comes home from work hungry; the meal must be ready... Sometimes he only has a few minutes to have dinner, because he has a class at the synagogue... Children grow up fast *Boruch Hashem,* they need new clothes, shoes, etc. To be able to cope with this busy schedule, our very dear wife needs many raw materials. The flow of production is incessant and under the pressure of time. We can understand why our Sages *z'l* said that arguments start at home when the bag of flour starts to empty.

The husband must manage to link his nature (his capabilities) with that of his wife (her needs). A common and serene dialogue must get them to agree on the family budget so that the wife can meet all of her obligations for the smooth running of the home, this famous just-in-time factory... Not to mention the necessities of *Shabbos* every week, the circumcision of a new baby, the *Bar-mitzvah* of the big boy or the marriage of the eldest, in joy and good humor!...

May *Hashem* fill us with blessings, *Amen!*

## *The advice of our Sages z'l*

The Talmud (Kesubos 59b) deals with the responsibilities of a woman in relation to her husband. Aside from the emotional side, marriage is a set of contractual obligations. Through the *Kesuba,* the husband has duties towards his wife. Equally, our Sages *z'l* decreed the role of a woman in front of her husband, all this for the smooth running of the home and the good understanding of the couple. When the path is well lit, especially by the light of the Torah, it is easy to avoid pitfalls.

The *Mishna* (cf.) teaches us the work which a woman performs in her home, namely: taking care of the milling of wheat, making bread, cleaning the linen, cooking, nursing her children, arranging the beds and taking care of wool, such as making thread or making clothes. Her merit is great, because the proper functioning of the home is on her shoulders, to ensure the happiness of her husband and her children. In her absence, it's a disarray. This is the reason why we must generously express our gratitude by complimenting her, whether it is the husband or the children, without any sign of dissatisfaction, because it would be ingratitude, that *Hashem* should preserve us from it!

The *Mishna* continues by exempting progressively certain duties from the wife who received as dowry one or more servants by her father, to the degree where she spends her day comfortably seated on a good sofa. However, the *Mishna* concludes that a woman must not remain idle, it would cause her boredom, which *Rashi ha Kadosh* translates as dementia. However in his commentary, Rav Ovadia Mi Bartenura tells us that she must prepare wine for her husband (at the time of our Sages *z'l*, the wine was so strong that it had to be mixed with water to make it drinkable), arranges his bed and washes his face, hands and feet, because these tasks can only be performed by his own wife. Rashi (Kesubos 61a) explains to us that these acts are not an obligation for her, but a good advice of comportment given by our Sages *z'l* for the holy children of Israel, so that her husband cherishes her even more, by the expression of her affection for her husband.

When peace (Shalom) reigns in a couple, they are serene and can fully serve *Hashem*. When their attachment is strong, full of affection, it brings better children into the world. In conclusion, the Divine Presence reigns among them, which brings *Kedusha* (holiness) followed by *Brocha* (blessing) into their homes, *Amen for all the children of Israel!*

### *The wrath of Moshe Rabbeinu*

On the orders of *Hakodosh Boruch Hu,* our master Moshe ordered the children of Israel to avenge the blood of the twenty-four thousand of their brothers who died in the epidemic as a result of faults committed with the women of Moav. "Avenge the children of Israel against the Midianites (Bamidbar 31)." Upon returning from the war expedition, Moshe became angry with the army officers... "Have you let all the women live? Behold, these caused the children of Israel, through the counsel of Balaam, to revolt so as to break faith with the Lord in the matter of Peor, and so the plague was among the congregation of the Lord..."

Thereafter, we notice something unusual in the text. It is *Elazar ha Kohen* who dictates to the children of Israel the *Halacha* (the law) how to purify the loot brought back from the war, in place of *Moshe Rabbeinu.* Rashi explains: "Because of his anger, Moshe forgot this law which he had taught to Elazar ha Kohen."

Even for a *mitzvah* of this importance, it was inappropriate for *Moshe Rabbeinu* to get angry, even more so for "orphans from orphans" like us, whether it be with our wife, our children, our family, our friends or anybody! The price of anger will always be too costly! Our masters *z'l* said of him who restrains himself, *Hashem* forgives him all his sins...

## *Our Masters of the Pardess*

The Talmud (Chagigah 14b) reports the story of four of our Masters *z'l* who entered the "Pardess". According to Rashi, they ascended to Heaven by pronouncing a divine Name. According to *Tosfos,* they did not physically ascend, but only spiritually. The use of the divine Name enabled their *Neshoma* to access and observe "Worlds" inaccessible to ordinary people. These are Ben Azai, Ben Zoma, Acher (the other – Elisha Ben Abuya) and Rabbi Akiva. They wanted to reach a very high spiritual level. According to the *Zohar* (Parasha Pekude), they wanted to perform the *Tikun* (repair) of *Adam Harishon's* fault at its source.

The *Vilna Gaon* explains, that their souls ascended into the world of "Yetzirah" by pronouncing a divine Name, in order to study the different facets of the Tree of the knowledge of Good and Evil. However, before reaching the good part in the world of "Yetzirah" which is called the "Inner Brain", it was necessary to go through "the path of Evil Forces", to be tested there, that is, respecting the prohibition of stopping there and observing it, it was only necessary to cross it as an obligatory passage. Three of the four Sages stopped there and observed, this is the reason for their fall under the Evil Forces (Klipos), only Rabbi Akiva neither stopped or observed. He entered in peace (be-Sholom) in the "Brain" in a state of purity, made the *Tikun* of all that he could repair and came out in peace (be-Sholom). The Talmud continues by teaching us the reasons which led to the fall of the three other Sages, namely Ben Azai who died, Ben Zoma who lost his mind and Acher, who became a heretic.

1. According to the Maharsha, Ben Azai became attached to the *Kedusha* to the point that he could no longer leave it. This is the reason for his death, as the *Possuk* tells us (Shemos 33-20): *For man shall not see Me and live.*

2. Ben Zoma was not sufficiently able to receive the abundance of spiritual light, which troubled him to the point of losing his mind, as the *Possuk* tells us (Proverbs 25-16): *Have you found honey? Eat so much as is sufficient for you, lest you be filled, and vomit it up.*

3. Acher failed to pass the test of seeing an angel sitting in Heaven writing the merits of the People of Israel. The fact that he declared that there are in Heaven two authorities, *Hashem* keeps us from it, led him to become a heretic. A person who is defective in his foundations, is able to make mistakes later. Commentators explain that his mother, during her pregnancy, ate idolatry sacrifice meat. His father educated him in Torah study because of the power of the Torah, it was not for objective reasons. The Talmud also reports that he studied secular and forbidden subjects, while singing inappropriate songs.

The Torah says (Bereshis 2-16 / 17): *And the Lord God commanded man, saying: "Of every tree of the garden you may freely eat; but of the tree of the knowledge of good and evil, you shalt not eat of it; for on the day that you eat of it you shalt surely die."*

"Even Ezra" explains that *Odom Harishon* was full of knowledge because *Hashem* would not have instructed an ignorant. Before the fault of *Odom,* according to our verse, Good and Evil were two entirely separate entities. His fault was to have mixed Good with Evil and not to be able to distinguish them separately. Indeed, the knowledge of Good and Evil as a single entity was previously completely unknown to him.

The purpose of our coming into this world is to repair the fault of *Odom Harishon.* How? By separating Good from Evil, that is, by freeing the "nitzotzos of Kedusha" (sparks of Holiness) imprisoned by the *Klipos,* by studying Torah and practicing its *mitzvos.* Doing so weakens the Evil Forces, which later liberate the *nitzotzos* of *Kedusha.* However, this necessitates a fight throughout our life against Evil, to attain Good; just like our Masters, who had to go through "the path of Evil Forces" without contemplating anything, to reach the *Pardess.*

The world we live in looks like this famous corridor. We have to work all our life to cross it without contemplating what is not necessary for us, while setting ourselves "points of light", like a fixed daily moment of Torah study in the morning and in the evening, praying with a *minyan* three times a day, etc. The "Yetser Hara" (evil inclination) is constantly present to prevent us from doing so.

The verse says (Bereshis 4-7): *sin rests at the door; and towards you is its desire, yet you can conquer it.*
Rashi explains: "Sin, that is to say the inclination to evil. He constantly aspires to make you stumble."
"Yet you can conquer it", how? "If you want, you will dominate it."

The "Sforno" explains to us that our "inclination" leads us every day to seek to satisfy a little more our greed for pleasures. He reports the Talmud (Sucah 52a) which teaches us that our evil inclination strengthens daily and that we can only fight it with the help of *Hashem,* as the *Possuk* tells us (Tehillim 37-32): *But Hashem will not forsake him in his hands.* On this subject, the "Chofetz Chayim" wrote in the "Mishna Brura" (Siman Alef, Halacha 4-26) **that a man must fix for himself a fixed time to study daily books of Mussar without exception,** whether in small or large quantities. Because, even if he is of a higher spiritual level than his friend, his inclination is stronger than him. The admonition and words of our Sages *z'l* are the spice that softens the *Yetser Hara.*

The Talmud (Kidushin 30b) explains the verse (Devarim 11-18): וְשַׂמְתֶּם – *vesamtem – and you shall put (my words in your heart),* commenting on it as follows: סם–תם – *sam tam* (a perfect medicine). That is to say, the Torah is an elixir of life that heals all diseases, may *Hashem* preserve us from it. It looks like a father who beat his son and applied a balm on the wound by saying to him: "As long as this balm is on your wound, eat and drink everything you want, wash in hot water like cold water and you will have nothing to fear. However, if you remove it, your wound will become infected." Thus said *Hakodosh Boruch Hu* to Israel: "My son, I created the Yetser Hara and I attached to it a "Torah of spices"(note: like a healing balm). If you study the Torah, you will not be delivered into his hands, as the *Possuk* tells us (cf.): "If you improve, you can get up". However, if you do not immerse yourself in the Torah, you will be delivered into his hands, as the *Possuk* tells us (cf.): *Sin rests at the door.* In addition, the whole occupation of *Yetser Hara* is directed to make you sin, as the *Possuk* tells us: *He aspires to reach you.* If you wish, you will dominate it, as the *Possuk* tells us: *But you, know how to conquer it!"*

The *Pele Yoetz* teaches us on the subject "Refinements" the following things:

It is known that the entire coming of man into this world and all of the exiles that we suffer is for the purpose of refining the sparks of sanctity that have been scattered among the outer physical shells. This is the fruit of our prayers, *mitzvos,* and study, and for this purpose a person should have intention. Likewise, a man should have the same intention with regard to eating and drinking, and all of the oppression, pain, deportations, and forced conversions that the Jewish People have endured in the exiles. All these events are a great benefit for this matter, and therefore a person must accept it with love. This is because everything is negligible compared to loving *Hashem* and to providing satisfaction before the Heavenly

Throne. There is no greater satisfaction than this refinement, because all of the souls and sparks of sanctity are a part of a divine spiritual entity. To what can this be compared? To a King whose children and cherished ones were taken into captivity and are imprisoned in a narrow, dark, and languishing place. Great is the suffering of the King! The person who redeems the sons of the King is bestowing an incredible kindness upon the King, and he will surely pay him a reward. Similarly, one can imagine, to the extent of our understanding, the connection to spiritual refinement. There is more ancient wisdom to discuss on this topic. From this, one can understand how great is the evil of the sinner, especially in regard to the wasting of seed, which causes the outer physical shells to "oppress" the holy souls and the sparks of sanctity to sink further into the depths of the shells. How much pain does such a person cause to the Holy One Blessed Be He and the divine Presence? Behold, those souls are like locked-up prisoners and they plead in a similar voice of one mortally wounded. The divine Presence screams (Yirmiyahu 8-23): "Would that My head be like water and My eye like a spring of tears, I will cry day and night on behalf of the fallen of My nation." About them King David said (Tehillim 79-11): "Let there come before You the moan of the imprisoned; according to the power of Your kindness, free those who are condemned to death." In view of this a man should tremble and faint, and he should run to do any *mitzvah* and flee from sin. He should be very careful when reciting blessings over physical pleasures. Through the blessings, refinement is accomplished on the food. Therefore, he must be extremely cautious to say them properly. If he is not meticulous, it is his own soul that he harms. All of one's actions should be for the sake of Heaven, on condition that he manages his commercial affairs with justice according to the Torah. Then the herald of salvation will sprout forth quickly in our days. Amen, so may it be His will! (End of quote.)

Now we know the reason for our coming to earth, namely to repair *Odom Harishon's* misdeed by separating Good from Evil. **In this case, we have a real purpose in life and throughout life, until our last breath.** Free time has no place. Either we study Torah or apply its *mitzvos,* or we occupy ourselves (for example work) to allow us to do both. Life becomes real happiness, whether in tranquility or difficulties.

## *Rav Elazar Menachem Man Shach zt'l*

We are at the time of the First World War. A wind of war blows across Europe, while the detonations shake our hearts. Advancing rapidly, the Russian army took possession of all the cities that crossed its path. With each conquest, there was only desolation and devastation. The population that suffered the most was of course the Jewish community...

People in combat zones were devoid of everything, just like miserable migrants. No one thought about their possessions or their homes they left behind, preservation of life was more important than anything.

When the residents of the town of Slutsek learned of the impending invasion by the Russians, great fear gripped the students of the *Yeshiva.* They knew very well that if the Russians discovered them, they would be in danger of death. Consequently, the students hired several coachmen and hastened to get onto horse-drawn carriages to flee.

There was no longer a single place in the carriages and the convoy was about to leave the city when suddenly, the voice of one of the students (our master the *Rosh Yeshiva,* Rav Shach *zt'l)* was heard: "One moment! I forgot something, I have to get it! He jumped from the carriage and ran to the *Yeshiva* building. The other students exclaimed, "We are in great danger! How can we afford the slightest delay! What could *Leizer* (short for Elazar) have forgotten in Yeshiva? He's a poor child!" They did not wait long. After a few moments, *Leizer* reappeared, out of breath. He was holding in his hands an old worn *Mussar* book, "Shaare Teshuvah" by Rabbeinu Yona.

"What? Is that what you forgot in the *Yeshiva?* For that you put us all in danger!?"

*Leizer* did not understand the reaction of his friends: "We are fleeing to save our lives, however King Solomon said (Proverbs 4-13): *Hold tightly to the Mussar (morals) without ever weakening, guard it, for it is your life. Mussar* is the life of man! Without this discipline, there is no reason to live and no reason to flee the Russian army! Now that this book is with us, we have a reason to live and a reason to flee the Russians! He stopped talking and immersed himself into studying this "old book"...

Made in the USA
Middletown, DE
30 October 2022